The

An Urban Military Company, 1837–1919

Cleveland

George N. Vourlojianis

Grays

THE KENT STATE UNIVERSITY PRESS

KENT & LONDON

© 2002 by The Kent State University Press,

Kent, Ohio 44242

All rights reserved

Library of Congress Catalog Card Number 2001038315

ISBN 0-87338-678-7

Manufactured in the United States of America

06 05 04 03 02   5 4 3 2 1

Library of Congress Cataloging-in-Publication Data

Vourlojianis, George N., 1947–

The Cleveland Grays: an urban military company, 1837–1919 /

George N. Vourlojianis.

p. cm.

Includes bibliographical references and index.

ISBN 0-87338-678-7 (pbk. : alk. paper) ∞

1. Cleveland Grays (Militia unit)—History.

2. Ohio—Militia—History. I. Title.

UA398.C54 V68 2002

355.3′7′0977132—dc21

2001038315

British Cataloging-in-Publication data are available.

Contents

To the memory of my father,
a U.S. infantryman of the Second World War

Acknowledgments

THIS WORK on a bit of Cleveland history began as a graduate Civil War seminar paper and developed into a dissertation under the direction of Dr. Frank Byrne, whose sagacious criticisms, never-failing encouragement, and limitless patience helped steer the work to completion. I owe a special debt of thanks to my old mentor at John Carroll University, Dr. George Prpic, and to Professors John Hubbell and S. Victor Papacosma of Kent State University for their wise advice and encouragement. Frank Tesch and Leslie Graham read through the manuscript on more than one occasion and offered sound organizational advice.

Next, I must thank Joanna Hildebrand Craig, Erin Holman, Perry Sundberg, Will Underwood, and the rest of the staff of the Kent State University Press for their professionalism and editorial acumen. I particularly thank Kirsten Lavell, who spent much time and effort working with the book's many photographs. And I'm grateful to the willing, helpful reference librarians and archivists at the City of Cleveland Archives; the Cuyahoga County Archives; the Ohio Historical Society Archives, Columbus, Ohio, the National Archives, Washington, D.C.; and the Western Reserve Historical Society of Cleveland, Ohio.

Finally, and especially, I offer tremendous gratitude to the Cleveland Grays, who graciously opened their archives and historic holdings to me. Grays archivist William Stark was especially generous with his time and advice. And members George Woodling, William Smrekar, John Jenkins, William "Billy" Hirsh, and a host of others contributed significantly to the writing of this book, offering moral support and other much valued help.

Semper Paratus!

Introduction

AMERICANS HAVE never liked the idea of maintaining a large standing army or the thought of being forced into military service. However, despite this antimilitary bent in our national psyche, an army had to be organized and manned.[1]

Article I, Section 8 of the Constitution recognized the militia, and the Militia Act of 1792 gave it its legal teeth. The Constitution placed the responsibility of appointing officers and prescribing training for the militia squarely upon the shoulders of the states, which often were unhappy about these new mandatory responsibilities. The organized or common militia had to be effectively administered, trained, and equipped. The procurement of arms and equipment was not only a time-consuming enterprise but also an expensive one. Service in the militia was also, generally, unpopular. Consequently, local politicians had no qualms about underfunding the militia or turning a blind eye to the enforcement of the law. The constitutionally mandated militia existed only on paper. As a consequence, in order to protect themselves from foreign invaders and bolster undermanned local police, groups of concerned, patriotic citizens in towns and cities throughout the country joined together and formed independent volunteer military companies.

The independent militia received no state or public support. State legislatures extended them statutory recognition. They purchased arms and equipped themselves with money from their own pockets. Because of this, membership tended to be drawn from the monied classes of the socioeconomic strata, the same group which owned property that might be at risk. Extra monies were donated by established members of the community. Leading local mercantilists became honorary captains in the independent militia. New members were screened and voted upon, thus adding to the social exclusivity of the membership. The style of their uniforms was inspired by European fashion, as were the names they chose: Cincinnati Rover Guards; Boston's Ancient and Honorable Artillery Company; Boston Fusiliers; Savannah's Chatham Artillery Company; New York Fire Zouaves; and Cleveland Grays.

The independent militia drew from the same pool of men from which the volunteer constabulary and the fire departments drew their prime movers and members. Their manly exercises fulfilled an assumed obligation of community stewardship, of Protestant noblesse oblige.

Independent militia companies were not, however, the exclusive domain of wealthy Yankees and Southern Cavaliers. During the first half of the nineteenth century, as part of an effort to combat nativistic sentiment, German and Irish Catholic immigrants banded together and formed independent military companies of their own. The main purpose of these units was to prove to their antagonists that they, too, were patriotic and loyal Americans. For many, military service helped open the door to respectability.

During times of national emergency, such as the Civil War or Spanish-American War, the independent companies lowered their stringent membership requirements substantially, so that their ranks could be expanded to meet the manpower needs of the conflict. After the crisis had passed and men returned to more peaceful pursuits, membership again became more selective. Still, egalitarianism would not be denied: the rosters now contained the names of a few Irish and Germans who had proved their worth in the company, perhaps under fire, and were now accepted as members. Also, these few were moving up the economic ladder and had the money to contribute to company military and social activities.

The independent companies had a social side that made membership in them attractive. These gentlemen's military social clubs sponsored lavish balls, extravagant trips and grand outings for themselves and their guests. On patriotic holidays they sponsored band concerts and paraded through the city streets.

The decades following the Civil War were a double-edged sword for the independent militia. The era of urban unrest and violence unleashed by the burgeoning labor movement increased the militia's role as urban police reserves. The local police were neither numerous enough nor strong enough to restore order and protect property. Many units of the ordinary militia—or National Guard, as they were now called—were sympathetic to the strikers and were not trusted by those in authority. Hence the government turned to the independent companies, who had not only a moral but a material stake in preserving order and protecting property. In many instances the businesses and property being threatened by the disorderly belonged to them.

But times were changing for the independent militia. While they were assuming a greater urban role, their national influence began to wane. America's increased role as a global power following the Spanish-American War necessitated centralization of administration and training of the military. The federally supervised National Guard replaced the independent companies. Independent companies had the choice of joining the National Guard or fading into oblivion.

The Cleveland Grays fits into the general pattern of such companies in American military history. Not a typical company, the Grays had a greater impact than most in their community—and they have survived.

Chapter One

"Success to the Grays!"

THE NORTHERN Ohio village upon which the State of Ohio on March 5, 1836, bestowed a city charter certainly qualified for the honor. Cleveland's population, made up largely of emigres from New England, already numbered nearly nine thousand. And the city's prospects were encouraging. It had been founded on a prime location, where the Cuyahoga River emptied into Lake Erie. Moreover, adding to the importance of the city, it was the northern terminus of the recently completed Ohio and Erie Canal, which gave it access to a vast inland empire. Cleveland's future looked bright indeed.

Cleveland's significance as a commercial center could be seen in its canal traffic: in 1836 more than 56,000 tons of freight arrived via the Ohio Canal in the bottoms of over nine hundred vessels that had docked at the port. No less important were the city's civilizing amenities. There were six churches; the city council had passed laws establishing schools, and as public institutions and enterprises were

5

founded, members of the community joined forces to form voluntary fire companies and a constabulary.[1]

However, as the population and commercial activity increased, so did the crime rate. Cleveland's *Daily Herald and Gazette* reported that crimes were being committed on an almost daily basis and clamored for the establishment of a city watch: "Will our city council . . . permit this to become a city of groggeries and a den of thieves?" In response to these concerns—preserving local order and protecting private property—a volunteer constabulary known as the City Watch was formed to deal with minor infractions of the law. Soon thereafter, the City Watch was supplemented by an independent volunteer militia company, which if needed could reinforce the local police. But during the summer of 1837, events in Canada exposed another need for a military company—defense against a foreign enemy.[2]

Fueled by economic depression and political discontent, an armed revolt against British rule broke out in the fall of 1837. The Canadian rebels, or Patriotes, called for the formation of an American-style republic. For over a year the revolt continued with fighting extending from the Niagara region west to Detroit. In March 1838, the British attacked rebel forces entrenched on Pelee Island in Lake Erie.[3] The revolt had now been brought almost to within gunshot of Cleveland.

On the American side of the border, newspapers called for action. While the *Daily Herald and Gazette* engaged in jingoist rhetoric, labeling the British as tyrants and likened the Patriotes to the "Heroes of '76," it also dutifully pointed out that the common militia in Cleveland was nonexistent. To remedy this situation, to be prepared should the fighting spread over the border, the paper called for the establishment of an independent volunteer militia company.[4]

With the need for a volunteer company established, the concerned citizenry had to band together and bring about its organization. The man who was to lead the movement to establish an independent company was Timothy Ingraham. A native of Massachusetts, Ingraham had been a member of a volunteer militia company at New Bedford. In 1832, at age twenty-two, he migrated to Cleveland. He became secretary of the Ohio Canal Packet Company and later was a principal in the firm of Standart, Ingraham and Company, forwarding and commission merchants. He served on the City Council as a Whig and was secretary of the firefighting Mutual Protecting Society.[5]

After several unofficial meetings, Ingraham gave public notice for an organizational meeting for what came to be known as the City Guards on August 28, 1837. Those interested citizens present elected principal officers, with, predictably, Ingraham as captain. Elected first lieutenant, or second in command, was Alfred S. Sanford, who, like Ingraham, had previous service in the independent militia. Before settling in Cleveland in 1829, Sanford had been a member of the Rochester Guards of New York. By trade, he was a printer. He was also very active in the volunteer fire brigade, and in 1845 he became Cleveland's fire chief. In 1833 Sanford married a widow, Mrs. Maria Hayward, who had a son by her previous marriage, William H. Hayward (Hayward would later have a distinguished military career and would serve as president of the Cleveland Grays and colonel of the 150th Ohio Volunteer Infantry Regiment during the Civil War). Benjamin Harrington was elected to the post of second lieutenant, third in command. Born in Vermont, he settled in Cleveland in 1835. He was proprietor of the Franklin House hotel.[6]

As the revolt in Canada gained momentum, so did Cleveland's oblique involvement. Out of a typically American dislike of the British at the time, Cleveland's general citizenry held meetings and established committees to collect donations for the Patriotes' cause. In early January 1838, Ingraham was appointed secretary of one of the committees responsible for distributing the collections to the

Captain Timothy J. Ingraham, founder and first president of the Grays, 1837–45. Ingraham was politically active and a prominent entrepreneur.

rebels.[7] Coupled with local considerations, the Patriotes rebellion had precipitated the formation of an independent militia company in Cleveland. The newly formed Cleveland City Guards increased their activities. The Guard formed committees to formulate a code of regulations, to solicit members, and to procure weapons, equipment, and an armory room. The by-laws and constitution established rules governing membership, uniform, and discipline. On September 18, 1837, seventy-eight men subscribed to the active company.[8] It is on this date that the Cleveland Grays can be said to have been founded.

Membership of the City Guard was limited to residents of the community "sustaining fair reputation." The roster of members reflected the composition of the city's middle and upper classes. The majority of the members of the Active Company were born in New England and were Protestants. Their average age was between thirty and forty. Of those listed in the *City Directory*, eighteen members were the proprietors of their own businesses or worked in family-owned businesses; seven worked in miscellaneous commercial enterprises; nine were tradesmen; five were printers; two were lawyers; two were clerks; one was a boatman; and one was a physician. Many of the men served, or would in time serve, the community as members of volunteer fire companies or by holding political office: three would be elected mayor; seven would sit on the city council; one would hold county office; and one would rise to the post of lieutenant-governor. Additionally, one member would serve on the board of directors of the Commercial Bank of Lake Erie, and still another would be appointed director of the Cleveland and Newburgh Railroad.[9]

An important adjunct to the membership was a provision for Honorary Members, the primary purpose of which was to increase the organization's treasury. These members helped the company purchase arms, uniforms, and equipment. An annual donation of five dollars or more secured Honorary status. In return for their generosity, Honorary Members were granted social privileges but were not permitted to drill or vote. On average, the Honorary Member was slightly older than the Active Company member. Of those listed in the *City Directory,* eleven were lawyers, ten were commission merchants, two were bookkeepers, and eleven owned their own businesses or were tradesmen. Much like the active members, many of the Honorary Members held, or aspired to, political office. Several became associated with the governing bodies of the city's banks and ever-expanding railroads. Of these men, six would become mayor; thirteen would be elected to the city council; three would serve as city attorney; one would become county prosecutor; two would serve as judges; and finally, one would be elected to the office of sheriff, one to the state legislature, and one to the United States Senate.[10]

Within the organization, order was maintained by a system of penalties in the form of fines. For example, fines were levied for infractions of discipline. Absence from roll call cost a commissioned officer fifty cents, a noncommissioned officer twenty-five cents, and privates twelve and half cents. For public intoxication or proof of dereliction of duty, the fine was two dollars. Public intoxication, making unnecessary noise, or smoking at meetings was prohibited. By vote of the company repeat offenders could be court-martialed and summarily dismissed. In an effort to maintain harmony and focus within the group, all political or religious discussions were "strictly prohibited" and any member who instituted the same was fined two dollars.[11]

The uniform adopted by the Guards consisted of a double-breasted coat with brass buttons and trousers "cut to fit the leg" and with a stripe of black cloth on the outside of the seam. Both coat and trouser were made of "cadet mixed," or gray cloth. The patent leather cap had a brass eagle on the front and was topped with a horse-hair plume. The motto adopted by the membership was "*Semper Paratus*—Always Prepared."[12]

Soon after its initial organization, the Company suffered a setback. Captain Ingraham was taken ill and remained in poor health for several months. During the time of his illness, drills and meetings were suspended. However, by the spring of 1838, Ingraham had recovered sufficiently to reinvigorate his creation.

In the meantime, by the spring of 1838, the British had successfully suppressed the Patriotes' revolt. Despite the removal of the threat of war with Great Britain the Company continued to expand its activities. On June 7, 1838, at their drill hall near Prospect and Ontario Streets, the members decided that the organization's name should be taken from the color of the cloth adopted for their uniforms—Gray. Henceforth, the company would be known as the Cleveland Grays.[13]

In July 1838 the Grays decided to order uniforms. Heads were measured for military caps, which were ordered from New York. With purchased cloth, the uniforms were to be made by tailor, and Company member, John Shelby. The men received their uniforms and hats sometime during the autumn of 1838. On Thursday, November 29, the Grays held their first parade. Formed in a single rank under the command of Captain Ingraham, the Grays marched through the crowd-filled main streets of the city "performing many evolutions with admirable promptness and skill." The *Herald and Gazette* lavished high praise on the Company. "Beautiful—Fine—Splendid! Just the thing for Cleveland. Fill up the ranks! Success to the Grays!" The *Herald* went on to exclaim that "They [the Grays] have shown that some things can be done as well as others in the West—that Cleveland, as well as Buffalo and Detroit can with justice boast of an independent corps."[14] Thus civic boosterism undergirded the martial spirit. With the Grays, Clevelanders, long considered to be on the edge of the frontier wilderness, felt a sense of participation in the country's growing feelings of nationalism.

The military company also had its social side. On December 24, 1838, the Company adopted a motion that the Grays sponsor a military ball. It was decided that "The Cleveland Grays First Annual

Ball" would be held the following January 23 in the assembly room of the American House, a hotel located on Superior Street. A committee of thirteen officers and men chaired by Captain Ingraham was appointed to organize the event. About four hundred "gentlemen and ladies, the talent and beauty of the City and County were present." Each couple paid five dollars, an amount equal to a week's pay for many working men. The hall was decorated in red, white, and blue bunting, and flags and portraits of Washington and LaFayette hung from the ceilings and walls. "The best music cheered them on . . . the sweet smiles and bright eyes of the ladies—the gallantry of the gentlemen," as the Gray's secretary recorded, "all combined rendered it a scene long to be remembered and never to be surpassed." At the conclusion of the ball, a special committee provided carriages and escorted the ladies home. The men then held a "stag dance" at which nonspiritous punch and cakes were substituted for spirits and tobacco, a tradition that thereafter closed each Grays ball. The Company sponsored five military balls between 1838 and 1842, and each of them was well attended.[15]

On May 22, 1839, the Grays held an encampment on Public Square. Charles M. Giddings, a member of the City Council and the board of directors of the Commercial Bank, presented the Grays with a standard. On one side of this banner, on a light-azure field, appeared an encampment of the Grays; on the opposite side was the Seal of the State of Ohio. Following the presentation there was a drill, and then refreshments were provided at Captain Ingraham's home. After yet more drilling, a reception was held that evening in the American House.[16] An important part of the life of nineteenth-century volunteer companies involved entertaining and being entertained.

On July 6 the Buffalo Guards, escorted by Frank Johnson's Philadelphia Brass Band, arrived in Cleveland by steamer at the invitation of the Grays. Attached to the company from Buffalo was an artillery or gun squad known as Fay's Battery. The spectacular drill and quick firing attracted such attention and impressed the officers of the Grays that soon thereafter the Grays obtained two bronze cannons and began organizing a gun squad. The gun squad was commanded by Sergeant David L. Wood, who had been a member of Fay's Battery and thus was familiar with the handling of artillery.[17]

In June 1840, the Grays traveled to Fort Meigs, in western Ohio, for an encampment with other Ohio and New York companies. General William Henry Harrison, Whig candidate for the U.S. presidency, was there for what was in effect an enormous political rally. During the War of 1812, Harrison had successfully defended Fort Meigs against two separate British attacks. The Company's presence reflected a Whiggish political bent. Northeastern Ohioans generally supported the Whig platform, which included an expansion of internal improvements, a protective tariff, support for educational reform, temperance, and the abolition of slavery. The Whigs, and to a lesser degree the Democrats, sent their political message with torchlight parades, mass rallies, barbecues, and jugs of hard cider. If available, cannon fire was added to the general hullabaloo. When money could be made, the Grays turned a blind eye to political loyalties. They were in fact very busy during the election of 1840; whenever either party held a political rally in Cleveland, the Company's gun squad was called on to add to the uproar by firing a salute. The fee for each firing of the cannon was fifty cents. (One such occasion, attended by Democratic vice president Richard M. Johnson proved to be singularly embarrassing to the squad: while Private Richard Dockstatter was priming one of the cannon, the powder flashed and burned off his whiskers.)

However, the enthusiasm of Clevelanders for their new volunteer company also proved to be short lived. July 4, 1844, marked the last appearance on the streets of Cleveland of the City Guard, another independent company that had assumed the Grays' original name.

Lack of interest and dwindling membership forced them to disband, members leaving to join the more glamorous and exciting artillery company. For these same reasons the Grays too faced dissolution. The death blow came early in 1845 when Timothy Ingraham left Cleveland and returned to Massachusetts. With their founder and principal motivator gone, in June 1845 the Grays began the sad task of disposing of their equipment and property. Much of the property was turned over to the gun squad, which had evolved into an independent company known as the Cleveland Light Artillery, and the uniforms and caps were sold to an independent company being formed in Painesville.[18]

These early years of the Cleveland Grays saw the establishment of patterns that would affect the activities of the organization throughout its history. First, the Grays were organized in response to a local exigency. Once the city developed economically and its population grew, there was an increased need for the maintenance of law and order. The increase in crime was countered by the formation of the constabulary, which was in turn bolstered by an independent military company. The organization of the Grays was also a local response to an external crisis: the threat of a third war with Great Britain as a result of American support for the Patriote cause. While muted and even nonexistent on a national level, along the Niagara frontier and the Great Lakes support of the rebels took not only rhetorical but material form. While giving the rebels financial and moral backing, sympathetic Americans indulged themselves by "pulling the lion's tail": if the British "lion" responded with military force, the city was ready to defend itself with its independent volunteer militia company.

Paradoxically, while the need for a militia force was recognized, very few of the citizenry were actively willing to shoulder a musket. The ordinary or common militia as created by the Constitution and mandated by Congress existed only on paper in Columbus. State equipment, uniforms, arms, and funds were either scarce or nonexistent. Thus, with no public source of support, the militia, in order to be effective, relied on volunteers who privately armed and equipped themselves. Money and equipment was raised by the company through dues, fines, special projects and donations. Of necessity, this circumstance decreed that the Grays would be composed of the economic elite of the community, who were, in fact, also the social elite. As a result, the Grays and other independent companies were removed from the common masses they had sworn to protect.

The second factor contributing to the establishment of the Grays was the presence of a strong personality. A crisis can stir the people's fears and elicit immediate responses. However, it is through the efforts and labors of a central figure or leader that the responses are crystalized into reality. The force behind the formation of the Grays was Timothy Ingraham. When he was active, the Company prospered and flourished; when he became ill, it languished; and when he departed for Massachusetts, it faded and disbanded. With recession and the decline of the crisis and the departure of the prime mover, the fickle citizenry withdrew their support of the Grays. The Grays remained dormant for nearly ten years. The expansion of slavery and the sectional differences exacerbated by the Mexican War gave rise in the North to a renewed martial spirit. Cleveland reflected this phenomenon.

Chapter Two

An American Company

IN THE DECADE before Abraham Lincoln's election to the presidency, Southerners feared that Northern interests, supported by social reformers, would gain control of the central government and declare slavery illegal. During the 1850s Southern fears gave way to full-fledged paranoia as Yankee abolitionists pressed for the full eradication of, or at the very least the containment of, the institution of slavery. As antislavery proponents pressed their agenda, Southerners began to arm themselves, making no attempt to disguise their intention to fight. However, the martial activity precipitated by sectional antagonisms, real or imagined, was not limited to the South. In the North, too, the tensions helped to stimulate volunteer militia activity. Activity in Cleveland was typical of the Northern urban reaction to what was happening in the nation. In the 1840s and 1850s sectional differences, together with the rise of the American party, or the Know Nothings, provided the impetus for the formation of several new volunteer companies in Cleveland.[1] Know Nothingism, which emerged from the urban North, was the political manifestation of anti-immigrant sentiment, or nativism. Economically, the nativists viewed the immigrant as a job competitor. Politically, they identified them as supporters of the Southern-dominated Democratic party. And caught up in this growing nativism and renewed military excitement was the reestablishment of the Cleveland Grays.

Cleveland's July 4th parade in 1853 bore witness to the citizenry's apparent military preparations and ethnic divisions. In addition to the various bands and civic societies, five military companies—the Light Artillery, the German Guards, the German Yagers, the Hibernian Guards, and the Washington Guards of Ohio City marched in the parade. Of the companies that participated in the parade, three were composed of ethnic Germans and one of Irish. During this period, as a response to nativist sentiment, the Germans and Irish founded their own military companies as a means of fostering their own ethnic identities while at the same time showing loyalty to their new land and culture. Many companies adopted American-sounding names to emphasize their patriotism. Despite their displays of loyalty, however, there was nativist reaction against these "foreign" volunteer units. Most of this hostility was directed against the Irish.[2]

In response to the increased number of foreign companies, nativists reacted by organizing their own "American" companies. What evidence exists strongly indicates that the Grays were reorganized as part of this reaction. Unfortunately, the Grays' records from the period 1854–60 have been lost; consequently, information must be drawn from other available sources, including newspapers, diaries, and regimental histories.[3]

In the late summer of 1854, a meeting was held at Ballou's Hall for the purpose of organizing a military company. Thirty-six men attended. The prime mover was Thomas S. Paddock, a dealer and manufacturer of hats, caps, and buffalo robes who had been a Gray in Ingraham's company and was a lieutenant in the Light Artillery. The new company chose the name Cleveland Grays.[4]

The formation of the "new" Grays was generally applauded in a *Cleveland Leader* editorial: "Well conducted Volunteer Militia are a safeguard and ornament to the city . . . furnishing a manly exercise for the members, teaching men to walk upright and firmly."[7] However, the Cleveland newspapers also noted that "the Know Knothings are not adverse to the formation of the new company" and pointed out that the company "is composed of Americans." In addition, in 1856 Thomas S. Paddock was elected to the city council as a Republican, a party that had attracted many former Know Nothings. During the presidential campaign of 1860, Paddock took an active role in boosting the Republican cause as a member of the Wide Awake Club. The Wide Awakes had distinctive uniforms and sponsored pro-Lincoln torchlight parades and rallies.[5] Members' political or ethnic orientation not withstanding, the day-to-day activities of the Grays centered around drills, parades, and target practice, the Company spirit seemingly more fraternal than military.

Following in the footsteps of the earlier company, the Grays, under Captain Paddock, held their first parade on January 22, 1855. The following July an encampment was held on the south side of the Cuyahoga River in University Heights (now known as the Tremont area). Camp Cuyahoga, organized to commemmorate the July 4th holiday, was jointly sponsored by the Grays and the Light Artillery and supported by six other Cleveland militia companies. Out-of-town units were also in attendance: the Chicago Light Guards and the First City Dragoons of Rochester. In August the Grays held another parade. The marching complement was ornamented by the daughters of Major David L. Wood of the Light Artillery and Captain Paddock; both girls dressed in the uniform of the Company and marched on either side of the Company flag carrying baskets of "rags with which to bandage the wounded and a cask of brandy for the fatigued and fainted soldiers," probably emulating the *vivandiers* popularized during the contemporaneous Crimean War and by the character, Maria, in the operetta *The Daughter of the Regiment*, which had been performed in Cleveland in the spring of 1855.[6]

As in 1837, one of the main purposes for the establishment of the volunteer militia was to support civic authority in times of local emergency. The only recorded instance of the Grays fulfilling this duty in the antebellum period was in the spring of 1855. At the request of Sheriff M. M. Spangler, a member of the 1837 company, a detail of six Grays stood guard in the jail the night before the execution of James Parks, a convicted murderer who had attempted to cheat the hangman by taking his own life. The Grays mounted a guard to watch the condemned man, who had been taken from his cell and chained to a bench in the hallway of the jail. Moreover, since there was some question of the man's guilt, the sheriff felt that the extra guards would discourage any attempts at a rescue. The day before the execution the Sheriff placed a notice in the newspaper: "Let all who have no business there stay away." The next day the sentence was carried out without incident.[7]

Early 1856 was active from several standpoints. Early in January the Grays were invited to Columbus to participate in the inauguration of Republican governor Salmon P. Chase, an invitation that further suggested the thrust of Grays' politics. At midmonth, the Company sponsored a concert, with brass band and glee club. Finally, at the end of the month, the Grays revived the tradition of sponsoring a grand military ball. And to celebrate Washington's birthday, the Grays, accompanied by the Light Artillery, journeyed to Cincinnati as the guests of the Rover Guards. After marching in the citywide parade, the participating companies retired to the traditional banquet at which each complimented the other with toasts and words of praise. On returning to Cleveland, the Grays paraded up Superior Street. "They never looked better," reported the *Leader*, "and after being dismissed they were invited to Richards and Hills Saloon, where they regaled the inner man."[8]

In March 1856 Captain Paddock and the Grays sponsored an event that illustrated the extent to which the martial spirit gripped the city. At the request of members of the community, Captain Paddock announced that a meeting of boys between the ages of nine and sixteen years would be held at the Grays' armory on Center Street for the purpose of instruction in drill and tactics. Captain Paddock viewed the enterprise as his civic duty, making the boys "better, more graceful and more manly" and thus better citizens. At the first meeting over 225 boys were present. They were organized by age into four companies. On May 27, after several practices, they held a parade. Newspaper accounts indicate that they were to appear again on the following July 4th, but the boys' company then disappears into forgotten history.[9]

But the Grays continued to grow, inacting changes in style and weaponry and leadership. In 1856 the Company adopted a new type of head gear: the tall, towering bear-skin cap became one of their distinctive trademarks. The *City Directory* of 1857 shows the Grays as having a complement of fifty-five muskets, described as "very elegant and serviceable arm[s]. Wishing to devote more time to his business, Captain Paddock withdrew from the active Company during 1858–59 and was temporarily replaced by William Henry Haywood. From time to time the Grays' busy social schedule was punctuated by military training. For example, in the summer of 1860 the Grays procured new minié-rifled muskets, and soon thereafter held a target practice, which was followed in the afternoon by a parade, which in its turn was followed in the evening by a full dress ball, of course.[10]

Part of the social life of the nineteenth-century volunteer companies involved drill competitions and exhibitions with one another.

Drill competitions were a community event. The military companies provided the entertainment and boosted civic pride in an era predating college and professional athletics. During the summer of 1860, for example, Elmer Ellsworth toured Northern cities with his Chicago Zouaves, a drill company inspired by the flamboyant French light-infantry soldiers stationed in North Africa. Ellsworth's company visited Cleveland in July and staged a drill exhibition. Impressed by the Zouaves' innovative, quick-paced drills, the Grays voted to adopt the dashing style, volunteering to drill two mornings and two evenings a week until they mastered the new style. However, before they were completely swept away by Zouave fever, Grays members voted to retain their traditional uniforms, shying away from the Zouaves' baggy red pantaloons and tasseled fezzes. Also, during this period the Grays introduced their distinctive and spirited "sky rocket cheer," a shrill whistle that crescendos to a "boom."[11]

Another community event led by the Grays was the commemoration of the Battle of Lake Erie by the unveiling of a monument to Commodore Oliver Hazard Perry on Public Square. The day's festivities included a parade and a sham naval battle and was topped off by a tremendous fireworks display.[12] This celebration marked the last peaceful gathering of the order soon to be shattered by the greater fireworks of civil war.

In the decades preceding the Civil War, a national tug-of-war had been taking place between those forces that wanted to expand slavery into new territory and those who wanted to contain, if not abolish, it. The new Republican party, led by the sixteenth president, Abraham Lincoln, was identified with those Northern forces that threatened slavery. Thus in 1860 many Southerners viewed Lincoln's November 6, 1860, election as a threat to their way of life. Some began to talk of secession.[13]

Recognizing growing tensions, militia companies in most cities, north *and* south of the Mason-Dixon Line, began recruiting campaigns to increase their numbers. Cleveland's military companies were no exception. Those that had supported Lincoln were willing to serve him and the Union.

On February 16, 1861, Lincoln stopped in Cleveland on the way to his inauguration. Upon his arrival at the lakefront rail depot, a procession was formed, with the Grays leading the militia escort, followed by the Light Dragoons and the Light Artillery. The president-elect was taken in an open carriage drawn by four white horses to the Weddell House where he was scheduled to speak. As the procession moved down flag-adorned Euclid Street, Lincoln was greeted by the cheers of his supporters. Banners proclaiming the sentiments and loyalties of much of the city's populace were draped from buildings along the route. One such banner read "Welcome to the President of Our Beloved Country—The Union It Must Be Preserved." At the Weddell House Lincoln was greeted by the dignitaries of the city, who welcomed him and pledged their unfailing support. In his remarks Lincoln spoke of the crisis the nation faced: "If we don't make common cause and save the good old ship, nobody will, and this should not be so." When Lincoln left Cleveland the next day, the Grays escorted him back to the railway station."[14]

By the time of Lincoln's arrival in Cleveland, six Southern states had made good their preelection threats and seceded from the Union. In the following months five more states withdrew.[15]

Chapter Three

ぐ

For God, Union, & Glory

On April 12, 1861, militia from South Carolina and other Southern states commenced firing on Fort Sumter in Charleston Harbor. One of the first shots was claimed by Edmund Ruffin, an ardent states' rightist and an honorary member of the Palmetto Guard, one of Charleston's independent militia companies. The Cleveland newspapers carried the sensational reports and responded with shots of their own. "Every life lost from the ranks of U.S. troops is laid down upon the altar of our country . . . and shall not be forgotten. The God of battle is with us, and will bring confusion upon our enemies."[1]

On April 15 President Lincoln issued his call for 75,000 volunteers to bolster the ranks of the army. The common militia existed only on paper, and the regular army of fewer than 16,000 men was scattered across the country, mostly west of the Mississippi. The president's call was followed by the states' issuances of orders mobilizing their militias. The largest military resource initially available to protect Washington were the Northern independent volunteer companies. The independent companies of Cleveland responded immediately to this call. Notices appeared ordering the Grays and the other Cleveland companies to their respective armories to await orders for possible deployment. Tension mounted as reports on the fate of the federal forts in Charleston Harbor arrived by telegram.[2]

On April 16, Brigadier General Jabez Fitch, commander of the Cleveland militia district and an original Gray of 1837, received word from the Adjutant General's Office in Columbus to have the Grays and one other infantry company raised to seventy-five men and prepared to leave for Washington on twenty-four-hours' notice.[3] The moment of truth for Captain Paddock and his Grays had arrived.

The Grays and their counterparts—the Sprague Zouave Cadets, the Hibernian Guards, and the Light Artillery—began campaigns to sign up recruits. At a rally held at the Melodeon Hall on Superior Street and presided over by Mayor Edward S. Flint, General Fitch challenged the able-bodied men of the community, telling then that "it should be the duty and aim of every good citizen to maintain the integrity and pride of our glorious nation." The speech was met with tremendous applause and wild cheering. The Grays' armory, or headquarters, located on Superior Street at Public Square, buzzed with excitement. A banner hung from a window proclaiming "The Constitution and the Union." Cheers for the Stars and Stripes and for the Grays resounded from the crowd gathered around their headquarters. Volunteers came forward and signed up. The Grays, thanking the crowd for their support, "responded with their 'sky-rocket' cheer."[4]

The business community as well as the citizenry supported those who volunteered. Employers came forward and announced that the volunteers did not have to fear the loss of their jobs while on active service. The Bank of Commerce offered to continue, during his absence, the salary of any clerk who enlisted. The Cleveland and Erie Railroad and the steamer *North Star* made similar offers to their respective employees who joined the Grays. The city's merchants raised a fund of five thousand dollars to care for the families of Grays away on active service. Cleveland photographers offered free photographs to any volunteer.[5] Lincoln's call for volunteers had taken on all the ballyhoo and hype of a political convention, or a latter-day championship football game. The scene was repeated in city after city across the nation.

At noon on April 17, General Fitch received orders to have the Grays and the Hibernian Guards, if at full strength, report to Columbus without arms by the first train. By the next day the Hibernian Guards had raised only fifty-two of the seventy-five required men. The Grays had exceeded their quota. It was decided that the Grays would proceed to Columbus; the Hibernians would follow as soon as they were recruited to strength.[6]

The officers and men of the Grays left Cleveland for Columbus on the afternoon of April 18. Prior to leaving, several of the men were presented with revolvers by their friends. After forming ranks at their armory, the Grays marched to the train station, escorted by Jack Leland's Band, the Sprague Zouave Cadets, and Colonel James Barnett's Artillery Battalion. A huge crowd of people lined the streets, and from every window or balcony or rooftop women and children waved handkerchiefs and flags at the passing troops. As the Grays and their escort approached the depot, Leland's Band appropriately struck up "The Girl I Left Behind Me." Upon arrival at the depot, the mayor and other city dignitaries made speeches, and members of the Cleveland Bible Society presented each Gray with a Bible. As the Company boarded the train, citizens placed "as tokens of sympathy for their mission in their hands paper money, gold coins and the like." The *Leader* reported that there were some painful partings, "but the Company bore themselves manfully." As the train pulled away from the platform, the band played "The Star Spangled Banner."[7]

The militia company that left Cleveland on that April afternoon in 1861 was in many ways different from that organized by Timothy Ingraham twenty-four years before. Their average age was now only twenty-three. And in order to meet the state's quota of seventy-five men, the Grays opened their ranks for the first time to the general public. In addition to Cleveland's elite, their numbers now included bank clerks, students, tradesmen, railroaders, saloon keepers, and a brewer.[8] The volunteers were young men, perhaps each with a different reason for signing on, but all in response to the crisis. Over half the Company was recruited during the three days following Lincoln's call for volunteers. As a consequence, most had probably never worn a uniform nor held a musket, let alone fired one. Even so, those who volunteered were made instant heroes by their neighbors, the newspapers, and the government.

Each town along the route to Columbus greeted the Grays with the same patriotic fervor. At Grafton a small cannon signaled the approach of the train; an American flag was suspended across the track, and the crowd gathered at the station sang "Columbia Must Be Free." LaGrange and Wellington also fired cannons and greeted the men with cheering and singing. When the train stopped at Shelby to pick up another company of volunteers, "There was a large crowd at the depot to see them off and much weeping among the female portion."[9]

Upon arriving in Columbus, the Grays and the Shelby Volunteers marched to Camp Jackson, a city park that had been hastily converted to a military encampment. There about a dozen companies were bivouacked—most without equipment and blankets. The Grays were billeted in the Supreme Court Room in the Statehouse, where some slept "on sofas, some in chairs, others were wrapped in their blankets and stretched out full length upon the floor with their knapsacks under their heads."[10]

That night Adjutant General Henry B. Carrington came in to thank the Grays for their promptness in volunteering and their loyalty to Ohio and the Union. He informed them that they would be leaving immediately for Washington and "would be assigned a position there corresponding with their merits." Their assignment was to the 1st Regiment Ohio Volunteer Infantry (OVI) as Company E. This regiment was composed of volunteer companies from all over the state.[11]

The regiment left Columbus by rail and arrived in Pittsburgh on April 20. In Pittsburgh, the Grays were billeted on a pair of river steamboats. "The Pittsburghers have treated us handsomely," wrote one of the men. "We have been victualed at the best restaurants in the city. The citizens would not allow us to pay for anything, even a cigar." After receiving arms at Pittsburgh, the 1st OVI moved on to Harrisburg and then to Lancaster. At Lancaster, the regiment was mustered into Federal service and Colonel Alexander McCook, an Ohio native and West Point graduate, assumed command.[12]

As the 1st OVI moved across Pennsylvania toward its destination, the scene back home in Cleveland bustled with the novelty of wartime activities. Grays "old timers" not only took charge of the Company's property and the armory, but they also made arrangements for the care of the families of the members on active duty. Captain Paddock, who was in New York on business when the call for volunteers went out, returned home and hastily made preparations to join his men in Pennsylvania. Before he departed from Cleveland, a group of local businessmen presented him with a brace of revolvers and one hundred dollars in gold as a token of the city's appreciation and admiration.[13]

The 1st OVI detrained in Washington on May 29. Soon after their arrival they were issued uniforms, equipment, and arms. Each man received one black felt hat with ornaments, one black pilot cloth overcoat, one blue flannel blouse, two red flannel shirts, one pair of pantaloons, and one pair of drawers. Originally armed with .69-caliber smoothbore muskets converted to percussion, the troops were rearmed with rifled percussion muskets. At this time the 1st and 2d Ohio were assigned to General Robert C. Schenck's brigade of General Daniel Tyler's division. Schenck, a native of Ohio, was a lawyer by training and a politician by profession. A Republican, Schenck had been an ardent supporter of Abraham Lincoln during the election of 1860; and upon the outbreak of the war, he sought an army commission and was commissioned a brigadier general of Ohio troops. Like many others whose appointments were in actuality political spoils, Schenck had no previous military experience.[14]

Not long after their arrival in Washington, the Grays saw the action for which they thought they were prepared. On June 16, four hundred men of the 69th New York Regiment moved by train down the rail line as far as Vienna Station, Virginia. Making no contact with the enemy, the New Yorkers withdrew. The next day, General Irvin McDowell, commander of the Union forces south of the Potomac River, ordered another reconnaissance in force from Alexandria, Virginia, to Vienna. The 1st OVI was selected for the job, with General Schenck in command.

The Ohio regiment left Alexandria by rail on the afternoon of June 17. Six miles down the railway line, Schenck passed the advanced outposts of the Union army and detrained two companies. At Falls Church, a distance of ten miles, two more companies were dropped off. The remaining companies, one being the Grays, continued on toward Vienna at slow speed, riding on flat cars preceding the locomotive and tender. While turning a bend in the right-of-way about a quarter-mile from Vienna, the train was fired upon from a distance of about four hundred yards by two Rebel guns dug into a hill commanding the tracks. The effect of the artillery fire was instantaneous. Schenck's startled men jumped from the cars and promptly took cover in the woods on either side of the track. In the ensuing confusion, and undoubtedly in an effort to save his engine, the engineer uncoupled the locomotive and withdrew, leaving the infantry stranded. The engineer's political sentiments are unknown. The deadliest effects of the enemy's fire were on Companies G (from Portsmouth), on the third car, and H (Zanesville), on the second car. Company E, the Grays, which occupied the front car, suffered one casualty; Lieutenant Joseph M. Richards was slightly wounded. Schenck lost thirteen men—eight killed, four wounded, and one missing.[15]

The unit that ambushed the Ohioans was the 1st South Carolina Volunteers, commanded by Colonel Maxcy Gregg, which had been dispatched to the vicinity of Vienna because of reports of Union activity in the area during the previous two days. Digging in at a bend in the track above the railroad, the Rebels prepared an ambush should the Union troops reappear. After the Confederates raked the train with shot and shell, the tremendous confusion and lateness of hour discouraged Union pursuit. The Rebels captured and burned the passenger car and five platform cars abandoned by the engineer.[16]

And so went the Gray's first action—ambush followed by near rout. The poor showing of the Union forces can be directly attributed to General Schenck's inexperience as well as that of the troops under his command. By definition, a reconnaissance, even in force, is a search, and as such is normally carried out with a certain degree of stealth. The manner in which the 1st OVI moved toward Vienna—on a train sounding its whistle—invited disaster. Maxcy Gregg, on the other hand, showed sound judgment in choosing the site for the ambush—a bend in the track—and by deploying his artillery and infantry in mutually supporting roles.

After the fiasco at Vienna, the regiment retired to a bivouac near

Alexandria. Here the Grays received their first pay, twenty-nine dollars in gold. Told there would be no immediate action, Captain Paddock returned to Cleveland to look after pressing business matters. (What these were is unknown.) However, he promised to return on time to accompany the Grays home when their enlistment expired. Lieutenant Joseph M. Richards, who had been wounded at Vienna, resigned his commission and also returned to Cleveland. On July 8 Colonel McCook called for new elections to fill the vacancies. Jeremiah Ensworth was elected captain, James B. Hampson 1st lieutenant, and John Frazee 2d lieutenant.[17]

As the expiration of the Grays' ninety-day tour neared, rumors as to the exact day of their release ran rampant through the camp. The *Plain Dealer* reported that "the boys are looking forward to the hour of their arrival at home with throbbing hearts." And in Cleveland preparations were underway to give the Grays the heroes' welcome they doubtless anticipated. A committee headed by Robert L. Paine, a prominent Cleveland attorney, was formed to make the necessary preparations and included members of other volunteer companies as well as the Ladies Aid Society.[18]

As the citizens of Cleveland made their preparations, so did General Irvin McDowell. On the morning of July 21, his Federal army moved to seize the key railroad junction at Manassas, Virginia, defeat the Rebel forces, and open the way for the capture of Richmond, the enemy capital. Tyler's division was to make a secondary or diversionary attack at the Stone Bridge, under which Bull Run flowed. In accordance with McDowell's plan, Tyler's division in column, with the 1st OVI in the van, set out from Centerville for the Stone Bridge.

The Grays and the 2d OVI's Cincinnati Zouaves were deployed as skirmishers, the Grays on the right and the Zouaves on the left. The Grays marched in column formation with a distance of five paces between ranks; the Company was about a quarter of a mile ahead of the main body. As they approached Bull Run, the Grays, led by Lieutenant Hampson (Captain Ensworth was ill and remained with the main column), continued their advance until they came into full view of the enemy, who were visible across the run preparing for battle. Carlisle's battery was moved forward, whereupon the Grays took up defensive positions to the rear of the guns. Here the Grays lay for several hours awaiting the arrival of the slow-moving main body of the division. When Tyler's column arrived at the Stone Bridge, the Grays were withdrawn to rejoin their regiment, which had taken up positions in the woods.

Schenck's brigade then consisted of the 1st and 2d OVI, with the 2d New York in reserve. Company F, 1st OVI (Cleveland's Hibernian Guards) was deployed as skirmishers. They cautiously advanced toward the enemy entrenched on a hill commanding the stream. The Hibernians began firing. Soon the brass barrels of cannon appeared on the enemy's earthworks, maneuvering for a better shot at the Ohioans. Upon seeing the enemy's preparations to fire, Colonel McCook ordered his men to fall back into the woods. As they retired, the Rebels opened fire with grape shot. McCook's men dropped to the ground. The shot passed over them but hit and killed several of the New Yorkers, who were, unfortunately, literally standing in reserve. As the Confederates loaded for another volley, McCook's men hastily moved out of range.

Colonel McCook moved his regiment through the woods back to a position along the Warrenton Turnpike. The green soldiers nervously noted that many of the trees had been stripped of their bark by the enemy's guns. As the day and the battle progressed, Schenck's brigade was ordered to provide protection for a company of pioneers attempting to build a bridge across Bull Run. As the brigade advanced, a masked, or hidden, battery fired on them. They fired badly, however, and their shots either fell short or passed overhead. The Rebel shots were silenced by counter–battery fire from Union guns. But fearing the renewal of the enemy shelling, Schenck withdrew his troops.[19]

Late that afternoon, Colonel McCook received reports that Rebel cavalry had crossed over the stream and was moving in his direction. McCook, unshaken by the report, exclaimed that "he didn't care a damn for all the rebel cavalry in Virginia." He deployed the Grays forward on either side of the road to repel any attack. The enemy did not appear.[20]

It was about this time that the Union rout toward Centerville, Virginia, began. Tyler's division was ordered to cover the withdrawal. Of Tyler's force, the 1st OVI was the last Federal unit to leave the field. The Grays had no idea what else had occurred that day or what the outcome of the battle had been. After marching well into the night, the regiment halted outside of Fairfax and bivouacked.[21]

Thus ended the first major battle of the Civil War. The Confederates were clearly victorious, but they failed to capitalize on their successful action by effecting a vigorous pursuit. The Confederate loses in killed, wounded, and captured numbered 1,981; the Union 2,645. Casualties for the 1st OVI included three killed, two wounded, and two missing.[22]

Immediately after the battle the Grays reported four missing and one dead. During the fighting Private Haskall F. Proctor was wounded in the leg, placed in an ambulance, and sent to the rear; during the retreat the ambulance was found overturned, the horses dead, and Proctor missing. Private James McLaughlin was also reported missing. It was rumored that another missing man, Private George C. Wise, was decapitated by enemy cavalry while on detached service with the artillery. And while Private Edward W. Umlauft was initially carried as missing, he rejoined the Company on the next day. When asked what his reason was for being absent, he replied that "the rest outran him." The one Gray killed in the campaign was twenty-three-year-old Private James E. Wheeler, who was accidentally shot in the leg, above the knee. He was evacuated immediately to a hospital at Centerville and then moved on to Alexandria, where he died. At first Wheeler's wound did not seem serious, but, as would be the case with tens of thousands of soldiers during the war, he died of an infection. The mass carnage that was to characterize the progress of the war, with vast numbers killed in a single battle, had not yet begun, and therefore young Wheeler was buried at home rather than in a mass site grave. Eight Gray's escorted Wheeler's body back to Cleveland, where, on July 28, 1861, an estimated five thousand people watched the funeral procession, led by the Grays, to Woodland Cemetery.[23]

Upon the end of their ninety days' service, the Grays were mustered out. On August 3, 1861, the Company returned home. A triumphal arch had been built on Public Square and was decorated with red-white-and-blue bunting. American flags flanked the center of the arch, where there was hung a large portrait of George Washington. Crowning the arch was an eagle holding in its beak a scroll with the inscription "Constitution and Union." The Mayor Flint read a proclamation issued by City Council honoring the Grays and thanking them for their valiant service. After the speeches the crowd ushered their heroes to the Weddell House for a grand dinner in their honor.[24] The welcome committee and the press ignored the return of the equally valiant, but Irish, Hibernian Guards.

On August 17, Haskall Proctor's parents received a letter from their son, missing since the Battle of Bull Run, with the news that he had been captured by the Rebels. At the end of October it was learned that McLaughlin and Wise were also begin held prisoner.[25] All the men of Company E, 1st OVI, were now accounted for. As a group, the Grays had been among the first to go to and then return from the Civil War's first major battle.

Upon being mustered out, even before they had returned to Cleveland, members of the Grays talked of raising a new company of volunteers, and a group led by Lieutenant James Hampson began a campaign to enlist a new company for three years' service. Hampson did rejoin the reformed 1st OVI, now a three-year regiment, and assumed command of Company D. In addition to Hampson's efforts, other members of the Grays recruited two companies for the 103d OVI in July 1862. During the course of the war, members of Paddock's original Company E served in a variety of regiments. However, as the war grew in scope and ferocity the efforts and activities of the Grays became somewhat intermingled with those of the eighteen infantry regiments recruited from the Cleveland area. In the years following the Civil War, the Grays identified themselves specifically with their service as Company E, 1st OVI, and with the 84th OVI and the 150th OVI.[26]

The 84th OVI was recruited in May 1862 as a three-month regiment. Two companies of this regiment were recruited by the Grays: Company D, under the command of Captain John N. Frazee, and Company E, commanded by Captain James Pickands. The regiment was organized at Camp Chase, Columbus, on June 7, 1862, and on June 11 it was ordered to Camp Lawrence at Cumberland, Maryland, where it was to help protect the vital Baltimore and Ohio Railroad, the primary rail link between Washington and Baltimore and the westward route into Ohio.[27]

In mid-June 1862, Major General John E. Wool had sent a message to Secretary of War Edwin M. Stanton warning him of the importance of posting troops to guard the rail lines and other lines of communication between Washington and Baltimore. He further reminded Stanton of the strategic importance of western Virginia. In response to Wool's concerns, Stanton ordered him to take the steps necessary to protect and defend the Baltimore and Ohio line. Thus the 84th OVI was assigned to Wool's command. But in addition to keeping the Union lines of communication open, the 84th OVI was to help prevent, or at least disrupt, the movement of contraband by Marylanders sympathetic to the secession and to counter the guerilla bands that were harassing Federal supply lines and communications.[28]

The regiment's primary mission at Camp Lawrence was guard duty. In his diary Private Henry Burnham noted the stopping and searching of canal boats in attempts to prevent the passage of salt into Virginia. Burnham, whose diary traces the regiment's movements and assignments, also described the 84th OVI's July 4th parade through the town of Cumberland. The reception was cool: "Cumberland was a d——m secession hole not a 'hanker' chief waved."[29]

Through the summer the regiment's pickets guarded the main supply routes south and searched for contraband. On August 12, Companies D and K, both under the command of Captain Frazee, were ordered to Spring Run in Hampshire County, Virginia. Henry Burnham proudly noted, "We are now encamped near the North and South branches of the Potomac." During their deployment at Spring Run, Captain Frazee's men were sent out on patrols to look for Confederate guerrillas, or "bushwhackers." On September 13, 1862, the entire regiment was ordered to New Creek to help repel an anticipated Confederate attack, an assault that never materialized. With the completion of 120 days' service, the 84th OVI was ordered back to Ohio and mustered out of service at Cleveland on September 20, 1862.[30]

In 1863, in compliance with the state militia law, the 29th Ohio National Guard was organized. Little is known about the activities of the unit, but what is known is that it was organized and dominated by the Grays. The principal officers, Colonel William H. Hayward and Lieutenant Colonel John N. Frazee, were Grays, as were the men of Companies A and B. During this period the unit's duties were primarily social and ceremonial; the 29th provided honor escorts for returning regiments and military funerals and held fund-raising balls and masquerade socials.[31] This would change in the summer of 1864, however, when toasts and parades were replaced by hardtack and grape shot.

By the third year of the Civil War, Washington, D.C., had become the most fortified place on earth. The city was encircled by thirty-seven miles of earthworks and buttressed with palisades, forts, and heavy guns. In order to provide more troops for his campaign against Richmond, General Ulysses S. Grant had stripped the Washington defenses of most of its available and seasoned troops. This shortage of men was noted in the capital with alarm, prompting President Lincoln to call on the governors of New York, Massachusetts, Pennsylvania, and Ohio to provide regiments for special one hundred days' service in the capital.[32]

In response to this call, the 29th Ohio National Guard enlisted and was redesignated the 150th Ohio Volunteer Infantry. Mustered into Federal service on May 5, 1864, the regiment left Cleveland on May 12 with a glorious send-off. The men were escorted to the depot by a contingent of police and accompanied by Jack Leland's Band. The streets were lined with cheering people, and American flags adorned the route of march. Wives and sweethearts waved their handkerchiefs. From Cleveland the 150th OVI proceeded to Washington via Pittsburgh. The scene along the route to Washington was reminiscent of the 1861 trip south. As the train stopped in Pittsburgh, people cheered. The women of the city treated the regiment to a great feast and filled the men's "brand new haversacks" to the brim with cooked delicacies.[33]

The regiment's reception was quite different in Baltimore, where, though somewhat subdued by an overwhelming Union military presence, the pro-secessionist sentiments of the majority of the city's white population had not changed much since 1861. But as the 150th OVI marched through the streets of Baltimore, the men were welcomed and cheered by thousands of freed blacks. William G. Gleason remembered "How the darkies shouted and cheered along the line. The white people seemed mighty scarce in Baltimore when Union soldiers marched through town."[34]

The 150th OVI arrived in Washington on the evening of May 13 and was assigned to the Twenty-second Corps for garrison duty in the forts defending the city's northern approaches. The regiment quickly settled into the tedium and humdrum of garrison life. Enclosed forts were placed at intervals of 800 to 1,000 yards, and in front of these fortifications trees were cut down and the land cleared of anything that could give cover to an attacking enemy or to sharpshooters. The men drilled three times a day and took instruction in the firing and maintenance of heavy artillery. To maintain a state of readiness, the men were constantly placed on alert, and at regular intervals the companies were rotated from fort to fort.[35]

There was some adjustment for the men of the 150th OVI. That summer temperatures hovered in the nineties. Many men—unused to army life or the excessive heat of the Washington summer—became sick. It was so hot in June that drills were cancelled. As many as ten to twelve men per day succumbed to the heat or some other malady and were put on the sick list. And of course there was the "chow," part of the universal experience of army life. One member of Company K described the rations in this way: "On my plate I found a piece of pork one inch square, half an inch thick, and a piece of boiled turnip. . . . But there was plenty of bread, and what in my inexperience I called coffee."[36]

When not on guard duty or drilling with the heavy guns, the soldiers occupied or passed the time with any number of simple diversions. Men organized Bible studies and "comb and Jews harp bands." Some gathered to sing songs; others settled into letter writing, cooking, and foraging or stealing corn from nearby fields. Conversations—no matter how they began—seemed always to get around to the heat, their hunger, the mosquitoes.[37] But the boredom and routine of garrison life for the Grays was to be soon broken by Confederate general Jubal Early.

Throughout the spring of 1864, the Federal army under General Ulysses S. Grant had been hammering its way toward the Confederate capital after fighting in the Wilderness, at Spotsylvania Court House, and at Cold Harbor—some of the bloodiest battles of the war. A Union victory now seemed possible. General Robert E. Lee, commander of the Army of Northern Virginia, knew he had to resist the Union threat to his capital, Richmond, so in the summer of 1864 he ordered Jubal Early to create a strategic diversion by attacking Washington.[38]

On July 5, Early, leading 10,000 men, crossed the Potomac. On July 9 he scattered Federal forces under the command of General Lew Wallace at Monocacy, Maryland. Two days later Early's troops stood at the gates of Washington. On the morning of July 10 the "long roll" of the drum was heard along the entire line. Every man was called to arms. Fighting began to the front and right of Fort Stevens on the morning of July 11. The Confederate skirmishers advanced to within 150 yards of Fort Stevens's walls. The Rebel fire was returned by Union pickets who had retired in good order to the safety of the ramparts. The guns manned by the 150th OVI at Fort Stevens were ordered to commence firing. The enemy scattered and was forced back about three hundred yards. For the remainder of the day the guns manned by the 150th fired into the Confederate lines. The artillery fire ceased at 6:00 P.M., but skirmishing continued long after dark.[39]

During their attack on the capital, the Confederates occupied two houses that afforded excellent cover for their sharpshooters. Evidently the Union attempts to clear the land in front of the forts was not as thorough nor as successful as they had thought, and in the course of the action the Confederates killed or wounded about thirty Union skirmishers. The guns of Fort Stevens were ordered to fire on the houses. After scoring several hits, one of the houses caught fire, and the Rebels fled to safer ground. On the afternoon and evening of July 12, reinforcements began to arrive at Fort Stevens. In response to calls for help, men from the Sixth Union Corps were detached from service with Grant at Petersburg and quickly moved to Washington. Six thousand veterans were soon in the rifle pits opposite Early's Confederates.[40]

After appraising the situation, Early retreated, realizing that his exhausted army did not have the strength necessary to capture Washington. Furthermore, additional Union reinforcements were marching in from western Virginia, and unless Early withdrew he could be caught between them and the Washington garrison. The Confederates began withdrawing on the night of July 12. The next morning Union skirmishers found the Confederate lines abandoned except for a few stragglers and those too seriously wounded to be moved.[41]

The total Union losses numbered about 250 killed and wounded. The Twenty-second Corps losses during the defense were twelve killed and sixty-one wounded. During their time at Washington, the 150th OVI suffered seven deaths: five died from disease, one was accidently killed, and one skirmisher from Company K died from wounds.

The 150th OVI was relieved of duty and left Washington on August 11, arriving in Cleveland three days later, where they were greeted by a large crowd of well-wishers and loved ones. After stacking arms on Public Square, the men were honored guests at a great feast (at which they were treated to "a liberal allowance of ale from Richards and Colemans Saloon"). The regiment was mustered out of service on August 23, 1864, after 110 days of service.[42]

The ranks of the 150th OVI included many men who would in the years following the war rise to prominent positions within the community: 1st Lieutenant Marcus A. Hanna of Company C would become, among other successes, a leader in the national Republican party; Private Edward O. Wolcott of Company D would serve as U.S. senator from Nevada; Private Nathan Perry Payne of Company C and Regimental Quartermaster Herman M. Chapin would serve as mayors of Cleveland; Private George K. Nash of Company K would sit on the Ohio Supreme Court and run for governor; Private Conway W. Noble of Company A and Carlos M. Stone of Company H would serve as common pleas court judges; Private Moses G. Watterson of Company F would be elected county treasurer; Private Peter H. Kaiser of Oberlin's Company K would be elected county solicitor; and Private Allan T. Brinsmade would rise from the ranks of Company H to the posts of U.S. attorney and Ohio senator.[43]

With the standing down of the 150th, many of the Grays returned to service with the reactivated 29th Ohio National Guard, which, in April 1865, carried out its last significant duty. This finale to the Grays' Civil War service was bittersweet at best.[44]

On April 14 fifty-six-year-old Abraham Lincoln was assassinated in Washington by John Wilkes Booth. Cleveland was one of the stops on the 1,700-mile journey to Lincoln's last resting place at Springfield, Illinois, and the 29th Ohio National Guard was chosen to be the first unit in the military guard of honor.[45] The nine-car funeral train arrived at the Union Depot from Buffalo, New York, just after dawn and then moved to the Euclid Street Station (present-day East 55th Street). A thirty-six-gun salute was fired as the coffin was removed from the train for its journey to Public Square. The 29th was drawn up in a line, with arms reversed in mourning. Sadly, some of the Grays present had been in the honor guard that had attended the president when he passed through Cleveland on his way to his inauguration in 1861.

The solemn procession down Euclid Avenue was led by the 29th and the Camp Chase Band with Colonel William H. Hayward, a Gray, in command. Upon reaching Public Square at about 9:00 A.M., an honor guard of the 29th was posted around the bier. It rained throughout the day, sometimes quite heavily. But despite the terrible weather, by late afternoon an estimated ninety thousand people had filed through the pagoda-shaped pavilion to view the president's open casket. At 10:00 P.M. the casket was closed and members of the 29th helped move it back to the Union depot and onto the train for its journey west.[46]

With the end of the Civil War, as the regiments of the state militia were reduced and disbanded, the Cleveland Grays were released from their obligations to protect and defend the State of Ohio, returning the unit to its status as an independent volunteer company.[47]

History notes that the Grays were the first Cleveland company to answer Lincoln's call. Upon completion of their initial ninety days' service, the Grays returned to duty either as individuals or as a variety of different units. However, after First Bull Run, while other companies fought in far-flung places and in some of the bloodiest battles, the Grays as an organization maintained a strong presence at home, carefully venturing from time to time into the backwaters of the war as a hundred days' regiment.

The Civil War advanced and embellished the prestige of the collective. During the period after Lee's surrender, service in the Union army was a prerequisite for holding political office. In Cleveland, not only service in general but service with the Grays in particular could do nothing but enhance one's electoral appeal. The returned veterans also formed a business and commercial network that provided the organization and its members with a variety of goods and services. Because of their Civil War service, the Grays redefined themselves as part of a new economic and political elite. Moreover, their experiences together in the army formed an almost mystical sort of fraternal kinship that permeated everything they did and touched. For these reasons, the last quarter of the nineteenth century marked the heyday of the Cleveland Grays.

Chapter Four

✵

Protectors & Policemen

By the end of the Civil War, Americans had had their fill of hardship and carnage. In the North, civilians and politicians alike clamored for the speedy return of their sons. The staggering death toll and the sight of countless maimed veterans helped contribute to a national malaise and a rejection of the military. Across the country participation in military organizations waned. The Adjutant General's report of 1869 listed the entire ordinary militia of Ohio as just two infantry companies and two artillery batteries. In an age in which joining fraternal and benevolent societies was the norm, the independent volunteer militia companies generally succumbed to the apathy toward the martial spirit. The Cleveland Grays were no exception.[1]

In September 1869 Thomas S. Paddock called a meeting of the "old members" of the organization for the purpose of rekindling interest in the Grays. The central figures were all veterans of the

Civil War and respected members of the business community: Paddock, C. W. Noble, Joseph M. Richards, and Jeremiah Ensworth. At a subsequent meeting committees were appointed and a code of regulations promulgated. On October 1, with thirty-eight men present, Paddock was unanimously elected captain; at the next meeting Frazee was elected first lieutenant. Once again the Grays were reformed and rejuvenated through the efforts of a central figure or prime mover; and as with the refounding of the 1850s and throughout the Civil War, this central figure was Thomas S. Paddock, ably assisted by John N. Frazee.[2]

After the election of officers, the membership turned its attention to the procurement of uniforms, equipment, an armory, and a meeting room. At the October 1 meeting members discussed the style and color of the company's uniform. Many of the former Union men present did not wish to return to the gray color of the prewar period. In fact, a discussion followed in which someone introduced a motion to change the name of the organization. Having survived a recent "rebellion," a number felt that, despite ties of history and tradition, the donning of a gray uniform was unpalatable. The motion concerning the color of the uniform was tabled for future discussion, but a motion made to keep the name Cleveland Grays carried. By the end of the month the company had adopted a blue fatigue uniform with a gray cap. The dress uniform's style and color was to be debated at a future date. Other, less controversial, organizational efforts went on apace. Meetings were to be held at the Grand Army of the Republic Hall near Public Square, and the Company leased armory space at Lymans Hall on Superior Street.[3]

As during the antebellum period, the company was composed of Active and Honorary Members. Those wishing to join the Grays were subjected to a rigorous screening process. The aspirant first had to be recommended by a member, who would turn over the applicant's name, qualifications, and address to the Standing Committee for investigation. If the committee's report on the applicant was favorable, the entire membership voted on admittance. If five members voted against him, the individual was rejected. Between October and December 1869, sixty-four men were accepted into the Grays as Active Members; three were rejected.[4]

During the early post–Civil War period the membership continued to reflect the Grays' general above-average socioeconomic status within the community. All the elected officers were veterans of the Civil War. All were professionals or businessmen. The majority of the Company were professionals or at the managerial levels of business. In other ways, though, the complexion of the organization was changing. During the war the organization had opened its ranks to meet enlistment quotas, resulting the admittance of select Irish and Germans, whose names remained on the Company roster even after the war. Because of their wartime service, some of these men had earned positions of trust and responsibility within certain parts of the established community. Having been so recognized by their peers, a few Irish and German Clevelanders began slowly to be admitted to the Grays.[5]

Arming and equipping the Grays was of utmost importance to establishing a functioning organization, and at the end of October 1869, John Frazee went to Columbus to see "how and on what terms arms and equipment" could be procured from the state. Upon returning to Cleveland, Frazee reported that the state would supply the Grays with arms and equipment *if* they joined the state militia. Lieutenant Frazee, acting as a representative of the Grays, politely rejected the offer.[6] Throughout the nineteenth century the Grays would continue to refuse offers from the Adjutant General's office to join the common militia or, later, the National Guard. They knew that if they did join the states' troops, they would come under centralized authority and subsequently lose their independent and historic privileged status.

On December 30 the Grays held their first postwar parade. Accompanied by the Germania Band, the Grays, dressed in regulation uniforms and carrying Springfield muskets purchased by the Company, marched from their armory to Public Square, where they demonstrated their proficiency in the manual of arms. It was a short but symbolic showing, and afterwards they returned to Lyman's Hall, "where the needs of the inner man were cared for."[7] Despite the lack of public interest in the military, the Grays had managed to hold the Company together and had even begun to reinstate themselves in the public eye.

Still, the Grays were not a public organization. During the 1870s, as the Grays paraded through the streets and entertained themselves, forces began coalescing that would ensure their continued prosperity and provide them with a renewed purpose. In the postwar period "class warfare" provided a new rallying point.[8] Just as the Civil War had provided purpose, definition, and substance to the Grays' existence, the growing labor and class conflicts found the Grays assuming the role of protectors and defenders of property and the law.

The growth of the Grays was a direct response to an increase in labor-associated violence in urban areas, violence caused by rapid industrialization and urbanization.[9] Organized and unorganized laborers across the land struck for higher wages, shorter hours, and better working conditions. In response to the apprehensions of the business community—in Cleveland and elsewhere—there was a general revival of interest in the militia and aggressive armory building campaigns.

Early in July 1877 the Baltimore and Ohio Railroad announced cuts in brakemen's and firemen's wages, effective on the sixteenth of the month. These cuts were yet another blow to workers who had been struggling to make ends meet since the bad times following the Panic of 1873. The bad economic times produced cutthroat competition and rate cuts by the railroads, followed inevitably by wage reductions. The railroad managers responded to the complaints of their employees by openly showing their hostility to the burgeoning labor movement by discharging organizers and those who dared serve on grievance committees.[10]

In Martinsburg, West Virginia, strikers bent on destroying railroad property and the common militia who were sworn to defend it faced one another. Disobeying the orders of their officers, two companies of the militia sided with the strikers. The incident was repeated in Pittsburgh as sympathetic militiamen fraternized with the strikers. As a result, federal troops and militia from Philadelphia had to be called in to restore order and to protect railroad property and the homes of management.[11]

The telegraph flashed the alarming news west into Ohio. Adjutant General Charles W. Carr ordered out the independent and ordinary militia throughout the state, especially along the principal rail lines. By July 20 Cleveland began to feel the affects of the strike, as freight and passenger traffic came to a halt creating a logjam of rolling stock. Within a week 250 to 300 sympathetic workers on the Lake Shore and Michigan Railroad struck for more pay. At the same time 225 freight handlers at the Union depot struck for the same reason.[12] Fortunately, meetings by these Cleveland strikers were orderly and nonviolent. It is difficult to ascertain whether the orderliness of Cleveland labor was due to the strong show of force by the police department or to the fact that the saloons had been ordered closed. By the beginning of August, the Lake Shore men returned to work with the promise from management that future grievances would be dealt with fairly. Striking firemen, brakemen, and engineers also returned to work.

Indeed, Cleveland got off lightly. In the areas where violence did erupt, the emotion-driven, but unorganized, railroad men were unable to sustain the momentum of their actions and ultimately proved no match for the "loyal" militia and federal troops. By the end of July, most railroad employees throughout the country were forced to return to work without gaining better pay or working conditions.[13]

The union that had begun to weaken during the Panic of 1873 was rejuvenated during the summer of 1877. But the strike helped feed the growing fears of business and industry that labor, with its large foreign membership and tendency toward violence, was a serious threat to the national well-being. The sympathy that some of the common militia showed the strikers helped create feelings of apprehension and distrust among the powers that be, suspicion that perhaps there was a conspiracy between the two groups. On the other hand, the independent companies, by the select nature of their membership, were identified as being loyal and could be counted on to defend the interests of the community whenever necessary, a factor that contributed to the revival of the independent militia movement.

As early as the spring of 1877, Cleveland's civil authorities and corporate leaders recognized that the depression of the early 1870s had created a volatile and perhaps even desperate situation for the average working man. In a letter dated April 21, 1877, Cleveland mayor William G. Rose asked Grays general James Barnett to take command of the city's military companies and make plans for them to help reinforce the police force in preserving order and protecting property in the event of labor violence. General Barnett agreed. As a former police commissioner and one of the ranking military officers in the city, Barnett neatly assumed the role of commander of loyal troops.[14]

The fears and concerns of the business community were put forth in a letter from Mortimer D. Leggett to Barnett in August 1877 in which he reminded the general of the need to protect the city and that there was a serious problem because the ordinary militia could not be relied on to do its duty: "If called out it [the militia] would be likely, largely to fraternize with the turbulent elements." Leggett's solution was to form the Cleveland Reserve, which would support the police in case of trouble. He also called for a private meeting of leading citizens who would be willing to help implement the plan. Who attended Leggett's meeting is unknown, but the its effect was immediate. In September 1877 a group of prominent citizens met and formed a volunteer cavalry unit, the First City Troop; and during the summer of 1878, the Cleveland Gatling Gun Company, armed with crank-operated machine guns, was formed.[15] Both of these units could be used very effectively for crowd intimidation and control.

In his annual message, Mayor Rose boasted, "I have no hesitation in saying that the military organizations of the city are capable of affording ample protection to the lives and property of our citizens in case of danger." To further bolster the Cleveland's defenses, the city built an armory in October 1879. Located at Champlain and Long Streets, across the street from the central police station, the armory—with "towers with lookouts and loopholes for guns which commanded the street to prevent the approach of a mob"—served as the headquarters for the city's military companies, including the Grays, who had three rooms for their use.[16]

As the oldest of Cleveland's independent companies, and with their president as the police chief, of the city's militias the Grays were the most trusted by the corporate-political partnership and were thus in the van of the army against anarchy. After the crisis of 1877, there was a slow but steady increase in membership as recruits from the managerial and professional ranks joined the Grays. In 1869 the Company numbered forty-nine officers and men; by 1876 the Company's size had increased to sixty-nine; and by 1886, the year following the second Rolling Mill Strike, the Company's strength consisted of 118 officers and men. As a result, in October 1896 the Grays changed their organization from that of a company to that of a battalion consisting of two companies—A and B—each with seventy-five men. The battalion staff numbered fifteen commissioned and noncommissioned officers.[17]

As labor unrest and violence increased, the corporate business community and the Grays forged a symbiotic relationship that continued into the early decades of the twentieth century. Business provided the funds and recruits the Grays needed to survive and grow. (As an example, in April 1878 the Grays received a donation of two hundred dollars from the Standard Oil Company and used it to purchase new rifles.)[18] The Grays reciprocated by being a bulwark against anarchy and the protector of the business community.

During the summers of 1882 and 1885 the city was rocked by strikes at the Cleveland Rolling Mill Company. In 1881 the majority of the Rolling Mill's skilled workers had joined the Amalgamated Association of Iron and Steel Workers, headquartered in Pittsburgh, and in May 1882 the union struck when management refused to submit to their demands. The company responded to the strike by hiring "scabs." Despite attempts by the union and the authorities to prevent it, violence aimed at the scabs erupted on June 5. Bowing to public pressure and corporate demands, on June 14 Mayor Rensselaer R. Herrick placed the Grays, the Light Artillery, and the Gatling Gun Company on alert at the city armory and two days later General Barnett assumed command of the units.[19] The companies were not used for street duty, but rather they remained in the armory guarding the weapons and munitions.

By the end of the month, the strike began to collapse, and General Barnett had the companies stand down. Labor peace was transitory, however, and three years later, in July 1885, Cleveland and the Rolling Mill were once again rocked by a strike—this time a more massive and violent strike.[20]

On July 1, 1885, William Chisholm, president of the Cleveland Rolling Mill Company, announced a 10-percent reduction in wages effective immediately. When added to the 17- and 20-percent cuts of the previous year, this latest reduction virtually slashed the workers' wages in half. Unmoved by the company's claims that the wage reduction was unavoidable because of a decrease in business and an increase in competition in the iron trade, the unskilled and unorganized work force, mostly Bohemian and Polish, began walking off the job. Rolling Mill moved to break the strike by resorting to an earlier tactic—hiring "scabs." Violence broke out when the angry workers used force to prevent the scabs and foremen from entering the mill. By July 7 over 3,000 workers were on strike.[21]

On July 6, 1,500 workers marched from the Polish neighborhoods of Newburgh downtown to Chisholm's office in the National Bank Building to present their grievances. Standing with an American flag, the workers demanded that Chisholm immediately restore their lost wages. He refused. From Chisholm's office the crowd moved on to City Hall and presented their grievances to Mayor George W. Gardner. Mayor Gardner called for calm. Chisholm called for military protection.[22]

Despite the mayor's call for peace, violence increased as activists urged the strikers to close down all factories in which Chisholm had an interest. The president of the H. P. Nail Company attempted to bar the mob of angry men from entering the building and was severely beaten.[23] Strikers forced the closing of the nail works and the Union Steel Screw Company.

The following day Mayor Gardner mobilized the local militia, putting the 5th Infantry (ONG), the Cleveland Light Artillery, and the Grays on alert. Captain John Frazee announced that he could muster only fifty men, because many members of his company were out of town because of the July 4th holiday, but a squad of eight Grays did stay on duty at the armory.[24]

By the end of the month the Grays were taken off alert, and at the end of September the strike finally ended with Chisholm's pledge to restore the June wage. The workers got what they wanted. But

In July 1899 a streetcar strike resulted in the Grays being called up. They encamped at the Brooklyn car barns on Pearl Road until the strike was settled.

their victory was hollow: Chisholm refused to rehire many of the Bohemians and Poles who had taken part in the dispute.[25]

The Grays were called out for two other great strikes before the turn of the century: the Brown Hoisting Company strike in the summer of 1896 and the streetcar strike of 1899. While throughout the Brown Hoisting strike the Grays remained on guard in their armory, during the streetcar strike they took a more active role in events. They were charged with guarding the Brooklyn car barns, removing obstructions from the tracks, and providing security for nonstriking motormen. An example of the sort of obstacles the Company faced occurred when the Grays prepared to leave the armory for duty in the West Side's Brooklyn neighborhood and the transport company that had been hired to carry their equipment refused to do so. The teamsters were sympathetic to the strikers. A bit irritated, but undaunted, the Grays put their camp equipment and tents on a streetcar and rode to the car barns. Another incident

Grays on strike duty relax near the Brooklyn car barns in July 1899.

took place on July 26 when a squad of Grays riding in a car toward the Brooklyn Bridge had stones thrown at them and were shot at by a hostile crowd. No one was injured; but the incident revealed that part of the community was hostile to the Grays and those they represented.[26]

The Cleveland Grays began to prosper in their role as protector, drawing into their ranks young men from the seemingly threatened classes. With more members and the support of the business community, the Grays became almost wealthy. Moreover, the banding together in a common military and moral cause created and nourished a certain esprit de corps, and membership was made even more attractive by the many social advantages and activities that were associated with being part of Cleveland's premier independent company.

Chapter Five

§

It's Fun to Be a Soldier

THE ESPRIT de corps of the Grays was evident during times of military activity. Their successful accomplishments in the field may in large part be attributed to the camaraderie and, indeed, brotherhood, the membership felt for one another. They were bound together by common military interest and by membership in the same socioeconomic class. The Grays provided themselves with a myriad of social diversions, most reflecting the wealth the members or their friends possessed. Even training was as much a social as a martial event.

Each fall a target shoot was held. In 1879 the Grays held their marksmanship competition in a grove at the home of member Joseph M. Richards, located on Euclid Avenue some distance east of the city limits. The Grays were accompanied by the Gatling Gun Company, with whom they enjoyed a warm friendship. The two companies marched to a prearranged spot where they rendezvoused with wagons that took them the rest of the way to Richards's home.[1]

Forty-nine Grays participated in the morning competition. Firing Sharps rifles, the marksmen were given a trial shot and five consecutive shots at a target two hundred yards away. Prizes—which included a gold medal, a silver cup, a box of cigars, and a ton of coal—were given for the best and the worst shot. After the Grays had finished shooting, the Gatlings proceeded with their firing. Upon completion of the shooting and the awarding of prizes, speeches were made praising the services and courage of the participants. Afterwards, the Grays, the Gatlings, and their guests were treated to a sumptuous eight-course banquet prepared by Mrs. Richards. Following the feast the companies gathered together and serenaded one another. Before departing the Grays gave "three loud hearty" cheers for their host and his wife. It was after 9:00 P.M. when the units marched back into town. The *Cleveland Leader* reporter assigned to the event wrote that "another joyous memory of a merry day spent had been added to their list of happy times."[2] The list of happy times was long and growing.

Each August the Grays held an encampment, the purpose being to hone their military skills and expose the members to the rigors of camp life. These ten-day encampments were held at Geauga Lake, Chippewa Lake, and Put-In-Bay, and in 1882 the Company began a tradition of holding their encampments at Lakewood on Lake Chautauqua, New York. A week before the Grays departed general and special orders and information were issued. The corporal of each squad was responsible for seeing that all equipment was properly packed and that each tent was provided with the following articles: gun rack, wash stand, bucket, mallet, and broom. It was further noted that "the gray dress pants are all newly pressed . . . and should, together with the dress coats, be carefully packed." No liquids or goods of a perishable nature were permitted in the mess chests. Individual members were to bring their own toilet articles "and have at least two celluloid standing collars." Instructions given in 1885 cautioned the men that since this was their "first outing with new broadcloth pantaloons . . . don't sit on the grass."[3]

Upon arrival at Lake Chautauqua, the Grays set up their encampment. The tents—including officers' quarters, staff tents, and a mess tent—were pitched in parallel lines forming a company street and each was floored and carpeted and provided with a fly or awning that served as a front porch. The mess tent, supervised by the quartermaster, was large enough to accommodate the Grays and their guests at each meal. Arrangements had been made for local hotels to provide the food and beverages as well as the chefs and waiters.[4]

Each encampment was given a name. The encampment of 1893 was called Camp Oriental in honor of the Oriental Commandery of the Knights Templars, whom the Grays had invited to Lakewood

On formal mess evenings, liveried waiters helped to make the festivities glow.

as their weekend guests. This encampment was also visited by the Cleveland Canoe Club and a reporter from the *Leader*. The following year the encampment was named in honor of Cleveland mayor George W. Gardner, who accompanied the Grays on the trip. Future camps were named for other prominent Clevelanders: the camp of 1897 was called Camp M. A. Hanna and that of 1915 Camp Myron T. Herrick.[5]

After the camp had been laid out, a schedule of training activities and camp rules was posted. A typical day began at 6:00 A.M. with reveille. This was followed by police call, surgeon's call, guard mount, squad drill, and company drill and then target practice and skirmish drill. Formal training was normally suspended in the early afternoon and replaced with organized sports, baseball being the most

This photograph shows Grays in various uniforms of the period,
circa late 1880s.

Grays training with other similar units at Lake Chautauqua. Here, about 1895, members of Mess 1 relax in front of their building. For some long-forgotten purpose, by changing the spacing between words one can read the lettering above the door as "One Eyed Riley."

popular game, but football and foot races also attracting a following.[6]

The Grays also spent time making mischief and lampooning one another. Mock drills were held using brooms and shovels instead of rifles. Members played good-natured pranks and tricks on each other after training had ended and after taps. A favorite was sneaking out of one squad tent and collapsing the tent of another while the occupants were inside asleep.[7]

Mess 7 at Lake Chautauqua was graced with "the ladies," probably about 1895.

The local residents were always glad to see the Clevelanders arrive. Accompanied by their band, the Grays were an impressive sight and added to the excitement of the summer season. Their presence drew other visitors to the area, which added to the coffers of the local economy. During the encampments the Grays Band held nightly concerts that were attended by local residents and hotel guests. In turn, to show their appreciation for the concerts and the Company's annual business, the Lake View House and the neighboring Kent House Casino gave balls in honor of the Grays. Indeed, for those members who could afford it, Lake Chautauqua was a picturesque and convenient escape. And Chautauqua's residents could take pride and comfort in the fact that the gentlemen-soldiers of Cleveland were ever watchful and maintained a high state of readiness.

The Grays' regional reputation and local associations garnered them an invitation to participate in northeast Ohio native James A. Garfield's inaugural parade. At the time, however, the expense of making such a trip was more than the Grays could afford, and they were forced to decline the offer. Upon hearing this, members of Cleveland's business community came forward and gave the Grays the money necessary to cover the expenses of the trip. Mr. Dan P. Eells led the donors by presenting the Grays with a check for $1,000. By the end of February, $3,150 had been donated for the trip. The 5th Infantry Regiment, ONG, generously loaned the Grays overcoats for the parade, and veteran members and friends donated cigars, liquid

While the much of the Grays' time at Lake Chautauqua was spent in serious training, the members also enjoyed rather whimsical activities.

refreshments, box lunches, and a barrel of apples for the train ride. So finally, on the evening of March 2, 1881, seventy-nine Grays, accompanied by a twenty-piece band and eight drummers, left Cleveland by special train. They arrived in Washington the following morning in the midst of a snowstorm.[9]

During the parade on March 4, the grand marshal, General William Tecumseh Sherman, ordered the Grays to a position immediately in front of the carriage containing Rutherford B. Hayes and Garfield. Through the slush and snow, the Grays proudly escorted the two presidents. Along the route of march people cheered and applauded as the Company passed. Captain John Frazee, the Grays commander, later remembered how "the boys were equal to the emergency [snow- and slush-covered streets] and conducted themselves in a soldierly manner that caused a high complimentary notice from General Sherman." After the parade the Grays escorted Garfield back to the White House.[10]

The Grays Band also trained and played for reviews and social events. Note the "Pioneers" in leather aprons at far left.

A Grays honor guard stands in Cleveland's Public Square at the casket of slain president James A. Garfield, September 1881.

The Washington trip had unanticipated benefits. The financial support of Cleveland's business community further cemented the bonds with the Grays. Moreover, the invitation was an honor not only for the Grays but for the City of Cleveland; failure to attend would have served as an embarrassment to the entire community. The Grays' participation was a symbolic representation of the power and influence that the city commanded in the late nineteenth century.

The euphoria of Garfield's inauguration did not last long. Six months later the Grays sadly acted yet again as part of the guard of honor over the remains of another assassinated president. The vacation-bound Garfield had been shot in the back at close range by a disappointed and disaffected Republican, Charles Guiteau, and had died of his wounds on September 19, 1881.[11]

After lying in state for two days in Washington, Garfield's body was brought to Cleveland, where a pavilion festooned with two carloads of flowers had been erected on Public Square to shelter the president's body. The Grays, in full dress uniform, stood guard in relays as nearly 150,000 people (virtually equivalent to the entire population of Cleveland) passed by the bier. On the morning of September 26, in a heavy rain, the long procession from Public Square to Lake View Cemetery slowly moved up Euclid Avenue. The Grays occupied a position in the Second Division.[12]

Happily, eight years later, the Company was again invited to march in an inaugural parade, this time that of Benjamin Harrison. On March 4, 1889, ninety Grays and twenty guests and a drum major and a twenty-three-piece brass band left Cleveland on a streamer-decorated special train.[13]

A heavy rain was falling when the Grays reached Washington. One marcher remembered, "We were drenched to the skin . . . we never lost our soldierly bearing and it was applauded frequently along the line of march" from the railroad station to their hotel. The next day the Grays marched in the parade and then returned home.[14]

The Amusement Committee had been instructed by Captain William C. Morrow, the Grays' commander, to arrange for fun while in the capital. He also instructed the committee to hold an informal "open house" at the hotel for Company members and visitors. In addition to their own party, the Grays were invited to receptions given by President Harrison, Vice President Levi P. Morton, Secretary of State James G. Blaine, and Ohio senators John Sherman and Henry B. Payne.[15]

The era of the great parades continued through to the end of the nineteenth century. In October 1892 the Company traveled to Chicago for the dedication ceremonies of the Columbian Exposition and World's Fair. Ohio governor William McKinley requested that the Grays act as his escort during the opening ceremonies. Mounted on a prancing black horse, the top-hatted McKinley proceeded with the Grays to the fairgrounds.[16]

Wherever they marched, the Grays brought credit not only to themselves but to Cleveland. They embodied all the virtues associated with a dynamic and robust America. They were honorable, dutiful, and loyal to the government, to themselves, and to their patrons. These values brought them not only financial support but also national notoriety.

On two different occasions, in 1895 and again in 1906, the Grays traveled to New Orleans, where they served as the escort to King Rex during Mardi Gras. The trips were made at the invitation of two Crescent City militia companies—the Continental Guards and Battery B, Louisiana Field Artillery—the Grays had entertained during a visit to Cleveland.[17]

In February 1895, after their annual Washington's birthday parade, the Grays departed for their first trip south since the war. The Grays arrived in New Orleans amid the cheers of a crowd and the

The Grays marched in a parade at the Worlds Columbian Exposition in Chicago, October 1892, at the request of Governor William McKinley.

booming of an artillery salute. Together with their hosts, the Continental Guards and Battery B, marched the Grays from the depot to the City Hall, where they presented the Clevelanders with a key to the city. During their stay the Grays were royally entertained by their hosts. They were admitted to private clubs and given complimentary tickets to all the city's theaters. This busy period of celebrating culminated on Monday, February 25, with the Mardi Gras parade.[18]

The New Orleans trip was the first of many long-distance excursions the Grays and their friends would make, with each trip more ambitious and glorious than the one that preceded it.[19]

Planning for a trip to the Pacific Coast started in the spring of 1902. The trip to California, to be made the following year, would cost eighty dollars per member. In order to raise extra funds for the trip to California, the Grays raffled off an automobile. A party of ninety-seven Grays and their guests left Cleveland on May 2 for a three-week tour of the West. En route, in Santa Fe, the Grays met President Theodore Roosevelt who was also on a tour of the Far West and Pacific Coast. During his speech at the New Mexico capitol building and during the parade that followed, the Grays acted as the president's escort. A photograph of the Grays saluting President Roosevelt appeared in the nationally circulated *Leslie's Weekly*. Then, journeying to the Grand Canyon for sightseeing, the Company again crossed paths with President Roosevelt, who invited the Grays to a reception in his private railroad car.[20]

On May 7 the Grays arrived in Los Angeles, where the Ohio Society of Southern California gave a reception and ball in honor of their home-state visitors. On the following day, the Company marched in the La Fiesta des Flores parade. Again, President Roosevelt was in the reviewing stand.[21]

Proceeding north to San Francisco, the Company was again the guest of honor at a banquet held at the landmark Cliff House by the

San Francisco Ohio Society. The next day, in yet another parade, the Grays marched alongside President Roosevelt.[22]

From San Francisco, the Grays continued north into Oregon. After a brief stop in Portland, they began their journey home. In Salt Lake City the Company was treated to a recital on the "magnificant organ" in the Mormon Tabernacle, and while passing through Denver they were entertained at a "smoker," a stag dinner, given by the Denver City Troop.[23]

At the general membership meeting of November 5, 1906, J. Edward Aylard, chairman of the Amusement Committee, announced that a trip to Cuba was being planned. Those present voted their approval and a date of February 1908 was chosen. The cost of this trip for active members was $70, members' ladies $110, and "outsiders" $165. On Washington's birthday 1908, fifty-eight members, twenty-five members' ladies, and eighty-eight friends departed Cleveland for Miami.[24]

Before arriving in Savannah on the morning of February 24, stops had been made at Murfreesboro, the Stones River National Cemetery, and Atlanta. Royal welcomes greeted the Grays entourage everywhere they visited. In Savannah, they were escorted by the Savannah Volunteer Guards and were shown the sights of the historic riverfront city, including the house used by General Sherman as his headquarters during the Civil War. In the evening, the Savannah Guards and the Savannah Yacht Club invited the Grays to an oyster roast and dance. The *Savannah Morning News* reported that "The gray and red of the guards intermingled with the gray and black of the Grays made a pretty military scene."[25]

The Savannah press seemed curiously impressed with the Grays' special railroad train. They reported that the kitchen car served meals on linen and china bearing the Company's name. They further commented on the "ensemble car" being fitted with a piano and a dance floor. Of particular interest was the "locker car," complete with stock and bartender, which was reported to have been "a customary part of each trip." From Savannah, the party continued south, stopping in Jacksonville, historic St. Augustine, and Miami.[26]

The mast and lookout tower of the battleship *Maine* was still visible above water in Havana Harbor when the Grays and their guests arrived on board the steamer *Halifax* from Miami. At the pier the Company was greeted by a delegation from the U.S. Army: Major Herbert J. Slocum, adviser to the Cuban army, and Captain Harry L. Gilchrist, of the medical corps. Before entering the regular service during the Spanish-American War, Captain Gilchrist had been a member of the Grays. A large crowd gathered as the Grays formed ranks and marched through the streets of Havana to their hotel. The Company was escorted by mounted police and the regimental band of the 27th U.S. Infantry. For four days the Grays, guided

Five Grays stand on and around a stack of cannon balls at Havana's Morro Castle, during a trip to Cuba in February 1908.

by Harry Gilchrist, toured Havana. They visited notorious Morro Castle, where a guide animatedly told them gruesome tales of Cuban patriots tortured to death by the brutal Spaniards, and were treated to the delights of the Havana Carnival.[27]

Returning to Florida, the party journeyed north to Daytona Beach to see the automobile races and then up to Augusta, Georgia, to visit with old friend John D. Rockefeller, who was "wintering" in Augusta. He and his personal physician, Dr. Hamilton F. Biggar, also of Cleveland, were at the depot when the Grays' train pulled in. Later, they hosted a "monster barbecue in real old-fashioned Georgia style" for the visiting Grays. At the barbecue, Rockefeller mingled freely with the Grays, calling many of the older members present by their names and introducing the Grays to Augustans as "my friends" or "my boys," which indeed they were. The Grays had served his interests—and the interests of big business in general—well during the labor strike of the late nineteenth century.[28]

The Grays visited the Civil War battlefields at Chattanooga, Lookout Mountain, and Chickamauga before returning to Cleveland on March 8, 1908. The reported expense of the sixteen days was $22,910.87.[29]

The great "Southern Trip" was not their last. In 1910 they traveled to Mexico, and in 1912 they returned to the Pacific Coast. And in response to challenge by a former Grays captain, Henry Shupe, the Company began planning a trip to Europe for the fateful summer of 1914.[30] The Grays *did* travel to Europe—but not until 1918, and then not in the pampered style to which they were accustomed.

The greatest and most significant accomplishment of the Grays during the years between the Civil War and 1916 was the building of their own armory. Since 1879 the Grays had occupied rooms in the City Armory on Long Street. At Long Street they shared the building with Cleveland's other military units. The Grays and their

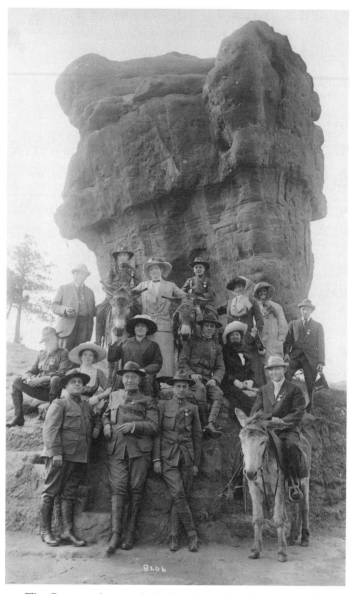

The Grays made several trips by chartered railway cars to the
American West after 1910. A group poses in front of an unidentified
landmark on the second trip in 1912.

benefactors perceived themselves as the premier Cleveland military company. In 1886, the leader of Cleveland's military community, General James Barnett, and the Grays began to discuss the possibility of building their own armory.[31] The impetus for building their own facility came not from a windfall donation but from a catastrophic fire.

On the afternoon of December 8, 1893, a man ran into the police station on Long Street and reported that smoke was coming from the upstairs windows of the City Armory across the street. Within minutes of the alarm, the building was engulfed by smoke and flames. Fire companies had just begun turning on their hoses when it was reported that ten thousand rounds of ammunition and two hundred pounds of gunpowder were stored inside the building. Despite the threat of explosion, the firemen remained at their hoses, now trying to prevent the fire from spreading to neighboring buildings.[32]

When the alarm was sounded the closest Gray was Otto Schade, who was working in his father's crockery and glassware business, the rear entrance of which was on Long Street. Schade ran to the burning armory and then into the building in an attempt to save Grays' property. After saving some of the bearskin shakos, he was forced back by smoke and flames. The gunpowder, which belonged to the Light Artillery, exploded and the armory walls blew outward. A large portion of one of the walls fell where, only an instant before, a crew of firemen had been working. Fortunately, there were no serious injuries.[33]

Members of the Grays searched the ruins on the following day. All that could be salvaged were the charred remnants of the organization's colors. Trophies of war, souvenirs, mementos, the Company's property—all was lost. Also lost was an original of Archibald Willard's painting *The Spirit of '76,* which belonged to the organization. The monetary loss to the Grays was calculated at about $25,000, $20,000 of which was covered by insurance.[34]

Not wasting a moment, the Grays held a meeting on the very night of the fire and voted to establish a fund for the purpose of building their own armory. At the same meeting a solicitation committee was appointed whose purpose it was to approach friends of the Grays for building subscriptions. In addition, all members of the Company were given a subscription book with instructions to begin canvasing their friends, business associates, and employers for donations. Meanwhile friends and comrades responded with offers of assistance and sympathy. Telegrams were received from the Louisiana Continental Guards and Louisiana Field Artillery. Locally, the Gatling Gun Company generously offered the Grays unconditional use of its armory.[35]

Plans for the building of the Grays' armory rapidly moved forward. On December 16, within two weeks of the fire, a committee was appointed to find a suitable armory site. By Christmas the building fund had received $12,494.50 in donations.[36]

In moves to repair the damage of the fire, the membership approved the purchase of new trousers and overcoats and ordered 175 stands of Sharps Rifles at a cost of $6.75 each. This was followed by the delivery of 125 bearskin shakos by the T. S. Paddock Company. Within six months of the fire, the Grays had replaced most of the military equipment that had been lost.[37]

The Site Committee reported in early February 1893 that it had "looked at property on Bolivar Street, next to the Church of Unity, with a frontage of 91 feet and 180 feet deep which could be obtained." Those present voted in favor of spending $17,950 for the lot on Bolivar Street.[38]

Fund-raising was not limited to outright donations. In addition to direct donations the Grays issued "Membership Certificates of Indebtedness," which in essence were bonds, though the Company could not legally issue bonds. The "Membership Certificates of Indebtedness" promised to redeem the face value on or before ten years at an interest rate of 5 percent payable annually. The certificates were issued in one hundred dollar and fifty dollar denominations, and members or friends purchasing certificates could make monthly installment payments of ten dollars. Many subscribers returned the interest to the Grays, and in some instances the money was used to credit dues. By May 1, 1893, the Solicitation Committee had raised $35,298.50.[39]

Since 1837 the Grays had been morally and financially supported by the business and civic communities, and in return the Grays had served them well. Corporate and civic leaders, some of whom had

Construction was begun on the present armory on Bolivar Road in 1893. This is the Grays' third building.

served in the Grays as young men, now came forward with donations for the armory building fund. Among the contributors was
James Pickands, who had fought with the Grays at First Manassas.
Well-connected, Pickands married Seville Hanna, sister to Marcus
Hanna, and in 1883 joined with Samuel Mather to form Pickands-
Mather and Company. Lord M. Coe also gave to the project. Coe,
who during the Civil War had been a member of City Council, was
president of the Cleveland City Forge and Iron Company and served
on the advisory board of Citizens Savings and Trust and on the
Chamber of Commerce.[40]

Other noteworthy contributors included Thomas H. White,
founder of the White Sewing Machine Company; William J. White,
the founder and president of the American Chicle Company (which
later manufactured Dr. Beeman's Pepsin Gum); Tom L. Johnson,
owner of the Cleveland Street Railway Company and later the pro-

The group laid the cornerstone for its armory on May 30, 1893.

gressive mayor of Cleveland; Marcus Hanna of the M. A. Hanna Company and a leader in the Republican party; and John D. Rockefeller.[41]

The cornerstone of the armory, which was cut from the sandstone quarries at Berea, was laid on Memorial Day 1893, which was a Civil War day of remembrance and thus had special meaning for the Grays and their friends. Inside the cornerstone was placed a copper box that contained Grays' medals and mementos, newspapers of the day, coins and paper money, letters, and a company roster. The main speaker was Judge Henry Clay White of the probate court. In his speech Judge White praised the Grays as being an important part of "an aristocracy of civic and social morality . . . which stands for social order and stability and public peace." He described the armory as "a school for patriotism and a citadel of social strength and sanctuary of safety in times of public commotion."[42] With its main turret and bartizans, the armory was designed to look like a medieval fortress, to impress upon the populace the power of the government and the military.

John N. Frazee, former commander and Cleveland's first police chief, was given the honor of placing the cornerstone. A hush fell over the crowd as the aging Frazee spoke. "I now lay the cornerstone of the Cleveland Grays Armory on the 30th day of May 1893 upon which a structure is to be erected in which I hope everybody will take an interest." Frazee then struck the stone with a mason's mallet. At the same instant the Grays raised a roistering three cheers and a loud roar, a "tiger." After the ceremony the Grays and their friends and guests repaired to the Gatling Gun Armory for a luncheon and celebration.[43]

The Grays Armory officially opened on the evening of February 12, 1894, with a drill. Their first banquet, held on February 22, celebrated not only Washington's birthday but also the fifty-seventh anniversary of the founding of the organization.[44]

This souvenir postcard depicts the armory upon its completion at the turn of the twentieth century.

The Armory drill hall ideally suited the military needs of the Grays. In addition, the large drill space also brought the organization some much-needed extra income. The Third Battalion, 5th Regiment, ONG, requested the use of the Armory for drills two evenings each month. The renting of the building to a unit of the National Guard also helped foster cordial relations between the organizations. The Armory was also rented for drill by the Knights of Pythias and the Knights Templars.[45]

Drill floor use was diversified and expanded in December 1894 with the purchase of a thousand chairs and a portable stage. Nine years later the Grays "modernized" the Armory, building a permanent stage house that could accommodate large productions. The

Theatrical fund-raiser entitled "The Streets of Cairo," sponsored by the Grays on January 22, 1894. All participants were members of the Grays.

Grays stand at attention in front of the Bolivar Road armory, prior to stepping
off for their birthday parade in 1904

basement was excavated for dressing rooms and storage, and a new
lounging room near the main entrance and a new ticket office were
installed. When completed, the new "music hall" could seat 2,200
people.[46]

The opening of the music hall brought increases in revenue and
prestige. Armory performers included the Metropolitan Opera, John
Philip Sousa and his band, the Philadelphia Philharmonic, Fritz
Kreisler, Ignatz Paderewski and John McCormick. Andre Sokoloff
conducted the inaugural concert of the Cleveland Orchestra at the
Armory on December 12, 1918. The Armory became so popular as a
concert hall that the *Plain Dealer* quipped that the Grays were "the

crack regiment that uses the Armory when concerts are not going on."[47]

The construction of the Armory resulted in some fundamental changes in the organization and nature of the Grays. The Grays were now the owners of real property and thus faced all the responsibilities and problems which are associated with property ownership. For the first time in their existence, the Grays were operating a business.

A new constitution was promulgated in April 1894 by which two separate organizations were formed. The traditional military company was joined by a parallel Civil Organization composed of a president, vice president, recording secretary, treasurer, and five-member

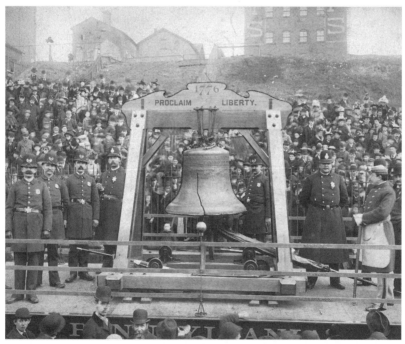

When the Liberty Bell toured the United States in 1893, Gray Conrad Mizer (lower right, wearing a leather apron) guarded the bell on its stop in Cleveland.

board of trustees. Grays' property, including the Armory, was controlled by the board, which was empowered to authorize all contracts and purchases. In the field or on encampments, the military organization's quartermaster could purchase supplies, but not above an amount allocated by the trustees. The new constitution also established rules of conduct within the Armory.[48] Simply stated, the Civil Organization was responsible for the business activities of the Grays.

The trips, encampments, and the building of the Armory were all manifestations of the Grays' changing persona. Their status in the community was defined and strengthened by their activities and associations. Wherever the Company journeyed, either hobnobbing with the president of the United States at the Grand Canyon or with the wealthiest man in the land at his Georgia winter home, the Grays were always welcomed as honored guests.

Chapter Six

Critics & Cuba

THE GRAYS were living up to the standards of conduct and expectations set by the portion of society from which their ranks were drawn. They were the darlings of the established society. They were not, however, always enthusiastically received by the rest of the citizenry.

Many regular army officers viewed the independent militias as incompetent, erratic, boastful, and wasteful. An officer assigned to the Ohio National Guard wrote that these militias served no useful purpose and actually were harmful to the National Guard; money and energies that could have been channeled to the Guard were instead donated to independent organizations. He further noted that there was no central authority to monitor their administration, training, and discipline and, finally, that "their practical efficiency is exhausted in their appearance." This officer found, however, the Cleveland Grays as a possible exception to his observations and indictments.[1]

At the Grays' request, in October 1895 this ONG officer inspected the Company. During the annual five-day encampment at the Armory, the Grays performed formations, drills, a guard mount, and a competitive target shoot for the critical eye of Captain H. O. S. Heistand, who was assigned by the War Department to the Ohio Adjutant General's Office. The *Cleveland Leader* reported that "hundreds of people who are interested in the military, persons representative of the society and fashion of the city were present" at the indoor camp.[2]

In his report, Captain Heistand was mildly critical of the condition of some of the weapons he inspected, but generally he praised the Grays for their excellent discipline, esprit de corps, drill, and high intelligence. He was particularly impressed with the "cordial good feelings" that seemed to exist among the local National Guard units and the Grays.[3]

These "cordial good feelings," however, were not consistently or universally shared by Cleveland's guardsmen or citizens. A National Guard officer commented after the Long Street armory fire that, when a new public armory was built, the Grays, as an independent unit, should not be permitted to use the facility. This attitude was consistent with some guardsmen's views that the Grays were elitist snobs and that the organization was more social than military. The *Penny Press* took pleasure in regularly lampooning the Grays, once featuring a mock advertisement under the headline "ENLIST": "Wanted for the Venezuelan army—637 colonels. The uniform is red coat, purple trousers with yellow stripes, green helmet and 16 yards of gold lace. Members of the Cleveland Grays specifically urged."[4] During the Spanish-American War, however, this sort of satire gave way to bald criticism.

In the early 1890s Cuba renewed its struggle for independence from Spain. In fierce retaliation against the Cubans, Spanish authorities herded women and children into concentration camps and punished suspected rebels in front of firing squads. When riots broke out in Havana in January 1898, President William McKinley ordered the battleship *Maine* to the Havana harbor to protect American lives and property. Shortly thereafter William Randolph Hearst's *New York Journal* printed a letter written by the Spanish minister in Washington, Dupuy de Lome, who accused McKinley of being a *politicastro,* or "small-time politician," and a "bidder for the admiration of the crowd." Americans were outraged by these insults against their president and anti-Spain sentiment exploded. Then, on the night of February 15, the *Maine* exploded and sank in Havana Harbor, with a loss of 260 American lives. A battle cry rang throughout the United States.

Congress declared war on the Kingdom of Spain on April 25, 1898.[5] President McKinley and his predecessor, Grover Cleveland, had tried hard to avoid war. For months, however, Americans had been treated to newspaper accounts of Spanish atrocities in Cuba, and the *Maine* disaster and the timely publication of the de Lome letter left no more room for diplomatic maneuverings.

The Grays quickly and dutifully volunteered for immediate service. During March and April 1898 discussions were held between Ohio's Adjutant General's Office and the Grays concerning their entry into the service as an active unit. The state's quota for infantry companies was already filled; but a new battalion of engineers, consisting of three companies, had been authorized and was about to be formed. On April 4 the Grays voted unanimously to offer their services as engineers.[6]

Members of the National Guard were critical of the entrance of the Grays into service as engineers. Major Arthur K. A. Liebich of the 5th ONG commented, "If the Grays wish to join the National Guard . . . they must be under the same regulations as all Guardsmen." Not mincing any words, Captain George McConnell of Battery A, 1st Ohio Light Artillery, made it clear that he had no use for special-privileged "tin soldiers." He said that "it would be a disgrace to permit the Grays to enter the National Guard. . . . Why should they have an easier time than the rest? . . . The Cleveland Grays is a social organization, not a military organization and should remain that way unless the members wish to stand on an equal footing with the rest of us." Others critical of the Grays accused Adjutant General Felix Axline of favoritism, and the *Penny Press* wryly observed that "Maybe, if the Cleveland Grays try real hard, they can get into the Salvation Army."[7]

Despite criticism and pressure from the National Guard, the Grays prevailed. House Bill 682 was passed by the General Assembly on April 21, authorizing the formation of a battalion of engineers at a maximum strength of 225 officers and men. In order to meet their enlistment quota, the Grays opened their ranks to new recruits. During the Civil War the Grays had recruited "suitable" candidates

The Grays were a unit of the 10th Ohio Volunteer Infantry during the Spanish-American War. Several Grays, wearing lighter colored uniforms, can be seen in this photograph of the officers of the regiment.

from outside the existing organization in order to meet the requirements for active strength. This same practice was successfully used in 1898.[8]

The Cleveland Grays were mustered into the Ohio National Guard as Companies A, B, and C, 1st Battalion of Engineers, on May 30, 1898, and assigned to the 10th Ohio Volunteer Infantry Regiment. The mustering officer was Assistant Adjutant General Colonel Herbert B. Kingsley. Grays' member Major Otto M. Schade was elected battalion commander. Company A was commanded by Captain James R. McQuigg, who had served with the 5th ONG but resigned in 1892 to join the Grays. An enthusiastic proponent of the Grays joining the National Guard as engineers, his energy and convictions were put to good use as the battalion recruiting officer. Company A was recruited to a strength of 105 officers and men. Civil War veteran and Grays member Edward N. Ogram was elected captain of Company B, which had a strength of 130 officers and men, and Company C was commanded by Captain Henry Frazee, the son of John Frazee, and numbered 108 officers and men.[9]

After weeks of anxiously waiting for marching instructions, the battalion received orders to report to Camp Bushnell, Columbus. At 5:00 A.M. on June 25, the battalion assembled at the Grays Armory. Some men wore their Grays uniforms, but the majority, who had been recently recruited, were in mufti. After roll call and breakfast, the 1st Battalion of Engineers formed ranks by company and marched out of the Armory.[10]

A steady rain fell on the Grays, who had now been joined by the Naval Brigade, as they marched to Union Station. The early hour and the rain discouraged most Clevelanders from gathering to cheer the volunteers off, though a few loyal citizens did line the streets as the guardsmen made their way to Public Square, where speeches were made and the Grays were presented with a stand of colors. Symbolically, Major Schade accepted the colors from Colonel

William H. Hayward, a Gray of 1837 and a veteran of the Civil War. Accompanied by the Great Western Band and the Naval Brigade Band, the battalion moved to the depot and boarded the train for Columbus.[11]

Soon after their departure for active service, the Grays came under sharp criticism from foes in organized labor. In early August, John J. Kinney, general secretary of the Metal Polishers, Buffers, Platers and Brass Workers Union unleashed a diatribe against the Grays accusing them of using "substitutes" instead of going to war themselves. The union leader argued that the majority of the membership had not responded to the call for volunteers as the Grays had claimed. With the exception of the officers and a majority of the sergeants, the ranks were filled with new recruits. Therefore, Kinney said, the organization should not receive any special privileges from the city. Specifically, he called for the recision of a city ordinance that authorized the payment of the salary for a janitor at Grays Armory. Doing so, he claimed, would mean that the city felt the Grays were no longer needed to help maintain law and order in Cleveland. Kinney continued his disparagement of the Grays by accusing them of cowardice. "They are not soldiers in any sense of the word . . . during labor troubles this organization always offered their services because they knew the poor half-starved fellows they had to face then did not have any weapons." Kinney's denunciation of the Grays was supported by similar comments from the Central Labor Union.[12]

The Grays refuted Kinney's charges. Major Arthur Foster explained that some of the men, including himself, could not leave their businesses for the extended period needed for active duty. Moreover, most members were married with families, some were too old for active service, and others could not pass the army physical. Therefore, in order to make up for the numbers lost and still serve their country, the Company had no choice but to conduct an aggressive recruiting campaign. The matter was dropped when Kinney could not muster enough support in the City Council.[13]

The troops were not prepared for what they encountered at Camp Bushnell. The camp had been hastily laid out, poorly planned. Many of the soldiers had no equipment, and there were shortages of uniforms, socks, and shoes. A steady diet of badly prepared food, unbelievably poor sanitary conditions, and inadequate medical care, together with the hot summer, wreaked misery upon the new recruits. The numbers reporting for sick call steadily increased. Some companies reported as much as 20 percent of their strength sick.[14] In an attempt to improve health conditions and sanitation, the camp was moved to higher ground in early August. The appalling conditions at Camp Bushnell were representative of the general lack of preparation of the army at this time, of an army not ready to go to war.

In mid-August, a week after the Spanish surrender, the 10th OVI was ordered to Camp Meade in Pennsylvania. Life was more tolerable at Camp Meade, which was under the command of the regular army and was well designed. The improved conditions were reflected in the shorter sick lists. Rations were still slow in arriving, however, and were never very palatable. The problem of poor rations became so acute that on more than one occasion Major Schade and his officers used their own money to purchase fresh vegetables and fruits from civilians in order to feed their men.[15]

The battalion drilled and learned military courtesy and discipline, training as infantry, not engineers. During the summer they spent their off-duty hours playing baseball and football, visiting the battlefield at Gettysburg, or fishing in the nearby Susquehanna River. But the change of seasons brought with it the painful realization that even though conditions at Camp Meade were better than those in Ohio, the battalion was still only partially equipped: the men had not been issued any winter clothing or tent stoves.[16]

In answer to their prayers for warmer weather, the 10th OVI was ordered to Georgia in mid-November, to the Second Corps at Camp MacKenzie on the outskirts of Augusta. The precision drilling and marching learned at Camp Meade were replaced with long marches three times a week. In the beginning the distance covered was six to ten miles; after a few weeks of conditioning, the marches were increased to fifteen and twenty miles. It wasn't until January, when new Krag-Jorgenson rifles were issued, that target practice was added to their training.[17]

Christmas 1898 was particularly lively and memorable and was welcome relief to the tedium of camp life. Squads went out beyond the camp to gather wild holly and mistletoe to be fashioned into decorations. Soon the entire camp was festooned with holiday garlands. The regimental quartermaster, Harry W. Morgenthaler, had designed and built decorative arches around the headquarters. The companies followed suit, each building an arch that bore the company designation and commander's name. During the holidays the soldiers received the customary packages from home and were supplied with delicacies and treats from the canteen fund. In return, the men went out into the cotton fields and sent home boxes of cotton as souvenirs.[18]

The overall lack of preparedness and planning that existed in the army manifested itself in the fact that most of the men and units raised never went to Cuba but rather remained in the United States. And so nine months after being mustered into federal service, on March 23, 1899, the 1st Battalion of Engineers was released and returned to Cleveland. Commenting on the Grays' contribution in the war against Spain, veteran Steve Sted said, "Nothing eventful took place but hard work."[19]

Not long after the Grays returned to Cleveland, a rift began to develop between those who had joined the Battalion of Engineers and those who had remained at home. Early in May a committee of twelve officers was appointed to formulate a plan for the peacetime

A most unusual snow storm in Augusta, Georgia, covered the Grays'
encampment at Camp McKenzie in late 1898.

reorganization of the Grays. Of the twelve members of the committee, only three members had seen service with the Battalion of
Engineers. Many of the members who had not served with the Engineers resented the Grays' identification with the National Guard.
With the conclusion of the emergency and their obligation met, the
majority of the Grays felt that the Company should cut all ties with
the Guard and return to its independent status. The committee recommended that the Grays return to the status quo ante bellum—an
independent infantry company.[20]

Later that month the Grays officers called a meeting with the
Engineers "for the purpose of recommending the officers of the Battalion." The Engineers preferred to be led by officers who had served
with the 10th OVI, not by Grays who had chosen to stay safe at home;

they claimed that it was their right to elect their own officers and that the Armory was their home too. After all, the members of the Engineer Battalion had been recruited as members of the Cleveland Grays.[21]

In an attempt to restore harmony and mend the widening gulf, Edward Ogram was elected captain of the Active Company. Despite this gesture and a partial reconciliation, ties between the Grays Active Company and the Battalion of Engineers were severed in August 1899. The Engineers were asked to vacate the Armory. The Grays returned to their independent status, and the Battalion of Engineers remained on the roster of the Ohio National Guard.[22]

The Grays had been expected to offer their services to the state during the crisis of the Spanish-American War, just as they had done in the War Between the States. But times had changed, and the nation was more complex than it had been during the Civil War. Groups of people whom the Grays had looked on as threatening the fabric of American society were slowly gaining political influence and media attention. There were now elements within the community that did not look on the Grays with the same favor and admiration of an earlier day.

Among the groups going through slow but positive metamorphoses was the National Guard. Better organized than it had been before, the Guard was now viewing itself with pride. Membership in the National Guard, by statute, was open to all. Further unlike the private militias, members were not screened prior to admittance. Indeed, the Guard rosters reflected all classes and backgrounds. As a consequence, these differences led many guardsmen and their officers to resent the more elite independent companies. And in Cleveland this anger was directed at the Grays.

The tone of relations between the Grays and the National Guard was in some part determined by personalities. If the senior officers got along well with one another, then there were "cordial good feelings." If not, the spirit of team cooperation was replaced by arrogant pretension and counterproductive rivalry. The Grays also found themselves the victims of those whom they were sworn to defend. In the newspapers and in the halls of government, unfriendly elements sniped at them and the order they defended.

The elitism and egotism of the Grays was quite apparent during the mobilization of 1898. The Grays rushed to the colors on paper, though the majority of the membership—for a variety of defensible reasons—chose not to (or could not be) muster into active service. To meet the quotas as they had promised, they opened their ranks and encouraged a mass of "outsiders" to enlist; however, once the emergency was over and their duty done, the established organization immediately voted to return to its independent, private status.

The negative publicity surrounding the Grays during and after the Spanish-American War, coupled with their shabby treatment of the Engineers, would not be easily forgotten. The *Penny Press* jeered, "If we remember the Spanish War, the easiest way to become a hero without risk is to join the Cleveland Grays."[23]

Chapter Seven

☙

Mexico & the Meuse-Argonne: Last Actions

AT THE END of the nineteenth century, a general spirit of reform spread over the country. Known as the Progressive movement, it affected all aspects of American life. Federal, state, and local governments passed laws regulating big business's activities and punishing its abuses. Municipal corruption was exposed and the guilty punished; civil service was professionalized and consumer protectionism addressed. Even America's army was caught up in a wave of Progressive reform and modernization.

The victory over Spain made the United States a global power. Now the army had to protect not only American interests and lives but distant territory as well. The military realized that it was only a matter of time before the United States came into conflict with some rival aggressive European or Asiatic power—a power with a modern, trained, efficient, and well-equipped army—and that they had to take measures to be ready for such a clash.

At the turn of the century, the U.S. Army began to take steps to reorganize and modernize itself into an efficient, centrally controlled force based on the European model. In order for the regular army to be able to act overseas as an arm of American foreign policy, as well as be able to protect the nation from invasion, it would have to be reinforced by a well-organized and well-trained National Guard.[1]

The first legislative step toward achieving this was the National Guard Act of 1903, or, as it was commonly called, the Dick Act, named for Congressman Charles F. W. Dick from Akron. In repealing the Militia Act of 1792, the Dick Act asserted federal control over the state militia by providing arms and equipment as well as supervision by regular army officers. The law prescribed minimum standards and times for drills, target practice and encampments. In addition, it stipulated that the president had the authority to call the militia into federal service for nine months. In 1908 the law was extended to permit the president to send the National Guard beyond the borders of the United States, and the time limits of service were removed as well. Federal control over the National Guard was strengthened further by legislation passed on the eve of the America's entry into the First World War. The National Guard Act of 1916 obliged Guardsmen to swear allegiance to their state and the federal government. In this act the president was given the authority to draft Guardsmen into federal service.[2] These series of acts, in addition to professionalizing and modernizing the National Guard, firmly established the legal dominance of Washington in time of war. State legislatures followed suit and passed bills that ensured that their National Guard organizations complied with the federal mandates.

During April 1904, the Ohio General Assembly passed legislation streamlining the state's National Guard. House Bill 398 decreed that all members of the state's militia were, henceforth, members of the National Guard. This bill also eliminated all statutory provisions for the existence of independent companies, a move that literally reduced the Grays to the status of a gentlemen's military social club. Ironically, the bill was signed into law by a Grays veteran, Governor Myron T. Herrick.[3] The Grays had fallen victim to the military's modernization.

Initially, the Grays were a bit dismayed by the action. Despite the fact that they had been virtually legislated out of existence, however, they continued their military training and social activities without interruption. At the business meeting on July 11, 1910, for instance, the Company voted to purchase new olive-drab fatigue or duty uniforms. (During the previous April, the uniform manufacturer in Cincinnati had sent a tailor to Cleveland to take measurements for the sample. As a practical joke, the Grays sent in Tom Hurley to be measured. As Hurley entered the room, the astonished tailor threw up his hands and cried, "Good heavens, how are we going to make anything on this contract!" Hurley weighed over 350 pounds.)[4]

As the modernization of the U.S. Army progressed, the Great Powers of Europe were readying themselves for war. On June 28, 1914, Archduke Francis Ferdinand, heir apparent to the Hapsburg throne, was assassinated by Serbian nationalists during a visit to Bosnia-Herzegovina. The archduke's murder triggered an unstoppable chain reaction that by the second week of August 1914 had plunged the nations of Europe and their colonial empires into the most destructive war up to that time.[5]

The war in Europe precipitated an awareness of the need for military preparedness. The sinking of the British passenger liner *Lusitania,* with the loss of 1,198 lives, including 128 Americans, jolted American public opinion toward the realization that it might be only a matter of time until the United States became a belligerent. Military preparedness became a popular and emotionally charged issue.[6]

Under the direction of the army's chief of staff, General Leonard Wood, a businessmen's training camp was organized at Plattsburg, New York, during the summer of 1915. Those who attended the four-week camp were encouraged to join state National Guard units.[7] The so-called "Plattsburg prescription for military preparedness" spread from New York to Ohio, with the Grays becoming the leaders of the movement in Cleveland.

After the enactment of House Bill 398, the Grays were no longer a recognized arm of the state's military forces. The passage of this law should have been a major setback for the Grays. However, as during past periods of civil disinterest and reorganization, the Company was always fortunate to have within its ranks a member who could, and would, provide the leadership and élan necessary to carry them through the crisis: in 1837 there was Timothy Ingraham, in 1852 and 1865 Thomas S. Paddock, and in 1914 Ludwig S. Conelly.

Born in Kingston, Ohio in 1883, Conelly moved to Cleveland as a young man and began a career in real estate sales and property management. He joined the Grays on September 1, 1903, and was elected captain eleven years later.[8] Conelly was an adroit and aggressive leader who seized the Plattsburg Citizen's Camp as the vehicle by which the Grays could still maintain a military presence within the community and redefine their purpose beyond that of a prestigious social club. Conelly steered the Grays on a course of preparedness.

Under his leadership the Company formed a rifle club and joined the National Rifle Association. Training was enhanced by the purchase of surplus Krag-Jorgensen rifles from Rock Island Arsenal in Illinois. In an effort to increase membership, the Company organized Armory Recruit Nights, open-houses where prospective recruits were introduced to the social and military roles of the organization. The Grays also decided to organize a training camp of their own. In late August 1915 Conelly traveled to Plattsburg to meet with

Captain Ludwig S. Conelly, organizer of the Grays' military training program at Chagrin Falls, relaxes while observing the exercises, September 1915. The camp was organized to provide military education for Cleveland businessmen.

General Wood. Wood told him that the army could not provide any material or financial support for the project but that a regular officer would be detailed to supervise the camp's operations.[9]

Upon returning to Cleveland, Conelly announced the Grays' intention of organizing a "Businessmen's Camp" following the Plattsburg example. The purpose of the camp was to provide business and professional men with the rudiments of an army officer's education. The camp idea was well received by the business and professional community, as both the former and the latter groups were bound to the Grays by historic ties. Cleveland mayor Newton D. Baker endorsed the project, and Colonel Charles Zimmerman, the commander of the 5th National Guard Regiment, offered his and his officers' services to assist in instruction and also offered the use of equipment and rifles if needed.

The project was not without its critics. Peter Witt, the progressive Democratic candidate for mayor, refused to support the camp, saying, "I am for peace and the way to have peace is to keep away from armaments." In spite of such comments, proponents of preparedness far outnumbered their opponents, and plans for the camp began in earnest. A recruiting office was opened at the Armory.

The camp would begin on September 4 and run through September 14 and be held at the county fairgrounds in Chagrin Falls. The cost of the camp would be about twenty-five dollars per man, a price that included a dollar a day for rations and a uniform cost of eight to twelve dollars. All other equipment would be issued at Chagrin Falls. The expense set the tone for the type of man who would be attracted and welcomed as a recruit, or "rookie."

On September 4, seventy-one rookies reported for duty. Among them were Cyrus Locher, county prosecutor; Pierce D. Metzger, county commissioner; Frederick H. Caley, secretary of the Cleveland Automobile Club; William E. Minshall, mayor of East Cleveland; George Loehr of Scribner and Loehr Jewellers; Daniel B. Cull, municipal judge; Stephen M. Young, state representative; and Raymond E. Munn, manager of the Cleveland Dental Supply Company. The fact that elections were only about sixty days away could not be overlooked; the camp provided a perfect venue for politicians doing their patriotic duty to gain extra media exposure.

True to General Wood's promise, the War Department assigned an officer to the camp. 1st Lieutenant James G. McIlroy arrived in Cleveland on September 1. On the first day of the camp, Lieutenant McIlroy appointed Ludwig S. Conelly second-in-command and divided the men into two platoons. Although the Grays had been legislated out of the formal military establishment, Captain Conelly had continued to lobby aggressively for some official military recognition for the Company. The assignment of a regular officer to the Chagrin Falls camp as an instructor was a form of such desired recognition.

A camp training schedule was posted. Mornings were spent learning the basics of the school of the soldier—discipline, courtesy, the manual of arms, and drill. In the afternoon the rookies learned weapons firing and patrol formations. Practical instruction was also given in compass reading, mapmaking, skirmishing over broken terrain, and trench construction. During these ten days, Cleveland lawyers, businessmen, physicians, and politicians came together and performed the duties of common soldiers.

The camp's importance and the prestige of the Grays may be gauged by the number of distinguished participants: Ohio Adjutant General Benjamin Hough; Governor Frank B. Willis; U.S. ambassador to France Myron T. Herrick; former Assistant Secretary of State Robert Bacon; Major Frank M. Fanning of the Battalion of Engineers; Congressman Henry I. Emerson; and retired army general Nelson A. Miles. But of all the important guests who came to the camp, the one visitor whose presence had a special meaning to the Grays was that of their former commander, eighty-five-year-old Colonel John N. Frazee.

Theodore Roosevelt had also been invited to the camp by the Grays. An ardent and very vocal proponent of preparedness, at a speech at the Plattsburg camp, the former commander-in-chief lambasted the Wilson administration as being soft on preparedness. Secretary of War Lindley M. Garrison reprimanded General Wood for allowing Roosevelt to make a speech critical of President Wilson's attempts at keeping the United States out of the war in Europe. As a result, talks at Plattsburg had been, by order, confined to military tactics and related subjects, and thus Roosevelt was unable to attend.

After ten days "in the field," Lieutenant McIlroy hiked the campers all the way back to Grays Armory, a distance of about twenty-five miles. It took two days for the Company to cover the distance; on the evening of the first day, the men set up a bivouac in North Randall. Once back at the Armory, the men checked their equipment and cleaned their weapons. After a brief inspection, participants were treated to a chicken dinner, during which a prize was awarded and speeches made. Victor Slayton, an associate editor of the *Cleveland Leader,* was presented with a gold watch for being the recruit showing special excellence. Henry P. Shupe, a past-president of the Grays, had offered up a five-dollar prize for the rookie most proficient at

Rifle marksmanship and "watching the enemy" were part of the regimen at Chagrin Falls, September 1915.

Grays greeted Ohio governor Frank B. Willis at the Chagrin Falls camp,
September 1915.

drill, but unfortunately the prize was not awarded because everyone
failed the test. During the dinner, Lieutenant McIlroy generally
praised the enthusiasm of the Grays and the camp participants.
Speaking of the merits of preparedness, he said, "I believe the camp
accomplished the work for which it was planned and the idea should
be encouraged if it will teach the public that a soldier cannot be
created overnight."

The need for trained officers and soldiers became more apparent
after 1913, when Mexican-American relations began to deteriorate,
reaching their lowest point since 1848. Revolution broke out in 1910
against the thirty-four-year dictatorship of Mexican president Por-
firio Diaz. President Wilson's subsequent interference in Mexico's
internal affairs, coupled with military intervention, resulted in a se-

ries of raids across the border by Mexican irregulars. In the predawn hours of March 9, 1916, Francisco "Pancho" Villa crossed the U.S. border with about 485 men and struck the town of Columbus, New Mexico, in a surprise attack. After a sharp fight in which eighteen Americans and between one and two hundred Mexicans were killed, Villa retreated across the border.[10]

American response was swift. In a reversal of policy, President Wilson ordered "an armed force [to] be sent into Mexico with the sole object of capturing Villa" and securing the border. Simultaneously, he called up the Texas, New Mexico, and Arizona National Guard units to help protect the border. And on May 11 Brigadier General John J. Pershing, commanding a punitive expedition of five

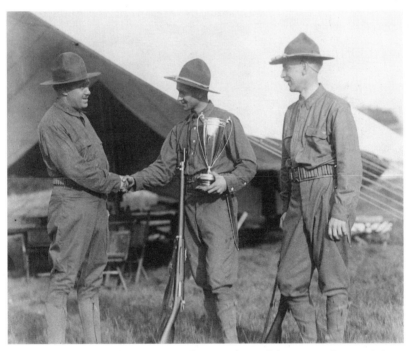

Marksmanship awards are presented to members of the preparedness training program at Chagrin Falls, September 1915.

thousand regulars, crossed the border in pursuit of Pancho Villa.[11]

Anticipating a general mobilization, Cleveland National Guard units began seeking recruits. Secretary of War Newton D. Baker and President Wilson issued a call for National Guard units on June 18, 1916. The next morning Adjutant General Benson W. Hough issued orders for the mobilization of the Ohio Guard.[12] The 1916 mobilization was different from past efforts in one important respect: independent volunteer units were now a thing of the past. Ludwig S. Conelly was painfully aware that despite their service history, the Grays had no official Guard standing. Nevertheless, Conelly was determined to raise a company of Cleveland Grays for service on the Mexican border.

The chance for action came—not from Cleveland but from the southwestern part of the state. The 3d Regiment, headquartered in

Grays, redesignated as part of Company F, 3d Ohio Volunteer Infantry, stand at attention in front of the State House in Columbus, summer 1916.

Dayton, was having difficulty finding enough volunteers to raise its Company F to official strength. Aware of Company F's manpower shortage, Captain Conelly opened a dialogue with the 3d's commander, Colonel Robert L. Hubler, with a view to mustering the Grays into his regiment. By the time of the Ohio mobilization, arrangements had been made over the telephone and by meetings between Colonel Hubler and Conelly for the Grays to volunteer en masse to fill up the ranks of Company F.[13]

On the afternoon of June 20, 1916, in a scene reminiscent of previous campaigns, Captain Ludwig S. Conelly assembled the Active Company in the drill hall of Grays Armory. As the Company was being formed and the roll taken by the first sergeant, the band struck up "Hail, Hail, the Gang's All Here," filling the air with excitement, pride and nervous anticipation. At 3:40 P.M. Captain Conelly ordered his men to "Right Face!" "Right by Twos, MARCH!" Forty-two volunteer officers and men marched out of the Armory onto Bolivar Road.[14]

Thousands of cheering Clevelanders lined the streets. Leading the march down Prospect Avenue to the depot, the band began to play a tune from another era of campaigning, "Marching Through Georgia." At the depot, the Grays hugged and kissed their loved ones and began boarding the train for Dayton. The last man to entrain was Captain Conelly. As the train pulled out of the depot, he stood on the car step raising his hat with one hand while holding a bouquet of roses in the other. Despite having been legislated out of existence, the Grays were, once again, the first private militia company to leave Cleveland during a call for volunteers.[15]

At the same time that Adjutant General Hough was issuing orders mobilizing the state's military, Governor Frank Willis appealed to the patriotism of the general citizenry and the business community. As in earlier call-ups, employers, anxious to show their enthusiastic support for the troops, pledged to continue the salaries and pay of soldiers and to preserve their jobs. Among the Cleveland businesses that made the pledge were the American Tobacco Company, Firestone Tire and Rubber, East Ohio Gas, and Bailey's Department Store. The most magnanimous gesture of patriotic fervor came from the management of the Erie Railroad Company, which announced that military service for employees would not be counted against vacation time. The Chamber of Commerce pledged to raise funds for the city's Guardsmen and to help care for their families.[16]

Knowing that the vast majority of the people back home supported them, the Grays set about the task of gaining the trust and respect of their new Dayton comrades. No doubt there were Dayton Guardsmen who resented the presence of the Grays in their regiment. Conelly and his men had to overcome feelings of mistrust, not only because of their historic privileged status but because they were from Cleveland, northeast Ohio. Once training began, the Grays were amalgamated with the regiment. On June 24 Captain Conelly received a letter from Major Daniel C. Stearns of the brigade headquarters in Columbus officially welcoming the Grays into the National Guard. He praised them for their quick mobilization and efficient movement from Cleveland which, he said, showed their sincerity of purpose.[17]

The Grays were dispatched to Middletown, where it was believed their presence would boost recruitment. The Grays marched into town headed by the 3d Regiment Band. Within a week, forty Middletown men had been recruited. To this list were added the names of fifteen more Cleveland men recruited by the Grays back home. While the Company was involved in recruiting, Captain Conelly was seeking funds to meet expenses. True to their word, the Cleveland Chamber of Commerce sent the Grays $350 to help defray the cost of mobilization and the purchase of equipment. The people of Middletown also contributed money for the welfare of the men.[18]

The regiment was ordered to Camp Willis in Columbus on July 3, 1916. The night before the Grays left Middletown, the streets were cleared of traffic and an outdoor dance was held. The Grays received another warm welcome from the people of Dayton as they returned from Middletown and marched directly to the depot. A cheering crowd estimated at 50,000 people gathered to see the 3d off to Columbus. Railroad cars were decorated with rousing slogans written in chalk: "Mexico or Bust!" and "To H—— With Villa!"[19] The 3d Infantry set off on what they hoped would be a great adventure.

But at Camp Willis everything changed. The appallingly unsanitary conditions and the lack of facilities were evidence that the Guard had learned nothing from the 1898 mobilization. Shortly after their arrival at Willis, soldiers, including several Grays, became sick with ptomaine poisoning. The cause of the outbreak was attributed to the mildewed bread, rotten beans, and nonpasteurized milk that was

Wives (or sweethearts) proudly display the Grays flag during the company's encampment at Camp Willis, Columbus, in 1916.

being fed to the troops. A cook told Colonel Hubler that he had been instructed to wipe the mold off the bread issued by the commissary. Hearing of the bad food and seeing some of their comrades sick, a number of Grays began sneaking out of camp and buying their meals at nearby restaurants.[20]

Responding to Colonel Hubler's loud complaints, Governor Willis came to the camp to examine the food. The governor pronounced the food fit for consumption by the troops. Unmoved by Willis's claim, however, Hubler pressed the issue of poor rations. The governor, not willing to risk a scandal, reversed his position on the food's condition and instituted steps to ameliorate the problem.[21] The poisoning stopped, but the palatability and quantity of the food did not improve.

In addition to being poorly fed, the regiment had not been paid. Colonel Hubler's requests and inquiries for pay were either answered unsatisfactorily or not answered at all. Troop morale began to ebb. In desperation, a frustrated Colonel Hubler appealed to Dayton's business community for a $19,000 loan with which to pay his regiment. John Patterson, president of National Cash Register, agreed to loan the regiment the money.[22]

The Grays, as Company F was proudly being referred to, were detailed as guards for the camp's provost marshal. While on duty, the Grays had to arrest thirty-two members of the Toledo Ambulance Company who had been caught raiding the gardens of neighboring farms and going door-to-door begging for food because they were hungry. Before morale could get lower than it already was, the regiment was ordered to the border. On September 7, 1915, the 3d Ohio, with a complement of 53 officers and 874 enlisted men, departed Camp Willis, making them the last Guardsmen to leave Ohio for the border.[23]

Ohio's infantry regiments were sent to Camp Bliss, near El Paso, Texas, and assigned to the Tenth Provisional Division. An Ohio

Guardsman described the camp's setting: "A level stretch of desert, absolutely free from smaller vegetation, with scarce a dozen trees growing upon it, extended along a dusty road for half a mile. The burning sun beat down upon the wastes and an occasional breath of scorching wind raised the dust and sand scattering it in stifling clouds along the plain."[24] The intense, unrelenting heat of southwestern Texas, which the scorpion and the armadillo call home, was a sharp contrast to the green landscapes of southwestern Ohio or the shores of Lake Erie.

The 3d Ohio was given no time to dwell on the miserable climatic conditions they found themselves in; training began immediately. Regular army officers supervised the training, which stressed range finding, patroling, land navigation, marksmanship, and weapons cleaning and care. To the school of the individual soldier was added battalion-and-company-size training and maneuvers. In October the regiment participated in what came to be known as the Las Cruces hike. Eighteen thousand Guardsmen marched seventy-five miles to

Grays on the Mexican border campaign in 1916 used White trucks, making them among the first troops using motorized transportation instead of horses.

Las Cruces, New Mexico, and back to Camp Bliss. The Guardsmen's rate of march was ten miles a day. The two-week march was
intermittently interrupted by deployments and measures designed
to counter the attacks of imaginary enemies. After this march the
members of the 3d Ohio began to view themselves as hardened cam-
paigners. (Their campaigning, however, would be limited, for no
National Guard troops crossed the boundary with Mexico; instead
they were kept on the American side patroling, providing guards,
and local security.) The novelty of the march was short-lived; the
regiment soon settled into the unglamorous routines of drilling and
inspections. The humdrum of camp life was only interrupted by
two-week rotations on border patrol duty. Considering the location
of Camp Bliss—on the hot, miserable Texas border with Mexico—
the general health of the men was good and food was satisfactory.
However, some of the men inevitably began to complain. To boost
morale, officers organized athletic competitions. Company F fielded
a football team and joined the outdoor basketball league.[25]

The Company's spirits were given a boost in late January when
Captain Conelly received a check for $108 from the Grays Veteran's
Association for the Grays' eightieth anniversary celebration. Officially, the *Plain Dealer* reported, the Grays on the border celebrated
the Company's birthday with a banquet and vaudeville show. In actuality, the party planned by Captain Conelly resembled a feast in
celebration of Bacchus more than the Grays' eightieth birthday. Based
on an account written by some Gray on the border, the Reverend
Hugh Birney of Cleveland's Euclid Avenue Methodist Episcopal
Church reported the evening's debauchery, at which liquor flowed
freely and a female dancer "clothed in nothing but a snake, wiggled
and squirmed about the hall, urged on in her performance by the
shouts and cheers of the assembled company . . . also a Hula Hula
dancer, exposed every muscle and fiber in her entire anatomy to the
beastlike gaze of the invited guests." The Reverend Birney had Cap-

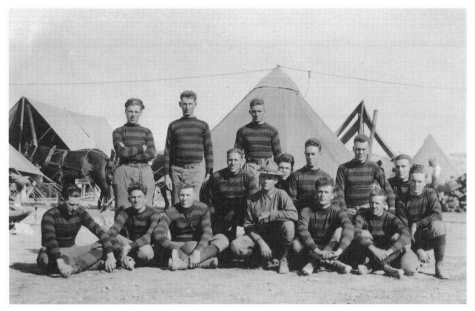

Members of the Grays football team pose for their picture while encamped near El Paso, Texas, during the Punitive Expedition against Pancho Villa.

tain Conelly's name, the names of his officers, and the entire Company removed from the rolls of the Baptist Brotherhood and the Cleveland Chapter of the Woman's Christian Temperance Union.[26]

Reverend Birney's source is unknown. However, several high-ranking officers present at the El Paso party were upset by the immoral display and were likely candidates. Portraying himself as an innocent victim in the affair, Major Frederick M. Fanning of the Engineer Battalion lamented, "My cheeks burn with shame whenever I think of the embarrassing situation into which I allowed myself to be led." Major Leon E. Smith, 1st Battalion commander, took a pious, but somewhat similar, position: "The shock was more than my constitution could stand. My only salvation was by turning to prayer. I have suggested that none of the Grays ever speak to me again. I have also suggested to Colonel Hubler that the Grays be transferred into another battalion." In the end cooler heads prevailed. "Under existing conditions," Lieutenant Colonel Carl I. Best, the 3d's executive officer, commented, "the less said the better."[27] Following Colonel Best's advice, Captain Conelly said nothing and the matter was dropped.

While the Grays Active Company was still busy soldiering on the border, keeping an eye out for Pancho Villa, on April 2, 1917, after exhausting all diplomatic avenues, President Wilson went to Congress to ask for a declaration of war against Germany.[28]

Back home in Cleveland, activities continued at the Armory under the direction of the Veteran's Association and the Civil Organization. Everything did not go smoothly, however. In early April the Grays refused to rent the Armory to the Socialist party for the staging of an antiwar rally. The socialists protested on the grounds that in the past they had been allowed to use the Armory for meetings.

Breaking with the tedium of camp life, this Gray clowns on the company street with his pistol in El Paso, 1916.

Grays colors on the banks of the Rio Grande, during the Punitive Expedition, 1916.

A crowd of about five hundred socialists and their sympathizers gathered at the Armory hoping to force the Grays into allowing them to hold their rally. They were met, however, by locked doors and a detachment of policemen who turned them away.[29]

Rebuffed, the angry leftists marched to Public Square, where, under the watchful eye of the Cleveland police, they held their rally. Their leader urged "workers not to join the Army or take up arms in order that Rockefeller, Morgan and Company may have their investments in Europe safeguarded and make more profits out of the munitions business." He further exclaimed that "Socialists cannot be made to fight!" Allowing the socialists to hold an antiwar rally at the Armory would have been an entirely inappropriate and unpatriotic action by the Grays, who were the stalwarts in Cleveland's preparedness movement and were presently involved in active federal service. (Later in the month at the Armory, former President William Howard Taft spoke on a subject more in keeping with the organization's activities, "Why Our Nation Needs a Strong Red Cross.")[30]

At the end of March 1917 the 3d Ohio returned from the Mexican border and was assigned to guard duty in various parts of the state. Company F, the Grays, was sent to Parkersburg, West Virginia, to protect bridges over the Ohio River from possible German sabotage. In August, in preparation for deployment to France, Ohio Guard units were ordered to report to Camp Sheridan, near Montgomery, Alabama, where they would form the nucleus of the newly organized 37th "Buckeye" Division. On September 27, 1917, the 3d Ohio was redesignated the 148th Infantry Regiment, 37th Division.[31]

While the regiment was switching numerical designations and coming under stricter federal control, the Grays were given a week's furlough. On October 1, the Grays arrived at Cleveland's Union Station and were greeted by an anxious crowd of well-wishers, friends, and family. The Grays of Company F, led by the Veteran's Association and the 3d Infantry band, marched from Union Station to Public Square to the Armory. There Captain Conelly ordered arms stacked and dismissed his men, whereupon the border veterans were rushed by the throng of onlookers. The citizens of Cleveland were quick to show their respect and appreciation for the sacrifices of their volunteers. The manager of the Hippodrome Theater, for instance, distributed free movie passes to the returning soldiers and their guests, and twenty automobiles were made available to chauffeur the Grays around the city. Finally, the Veteran's Association sponsored a clam bake and dance to welcome the Active Company home.[32]

Their furlough was very brief. On October 21, 1917, the 148th Infantry left Camp Sherman near Chillicothe, Ohio, for Camp Sheridan in Alabama. It was the last regiment to join the newly constituted division.[33]

Soon after their arrival at Camp Sheridan, members of Captain Conelly's original company began to be transferred to other units. Many men were sent to officer training schools, for the rapidly expanding army needed officers with previous military experience, even if this experience was limited to six months' duty on the Mexican border. (Of the seventy-eight men who served on the border with Company F, forty-two received commissions by war's end.[34]) With these transfers and promotions the emphasis of Grays participation in the World War shifted from the activities of Company F to the activities of Captain Conelly. Conelly's wartime experiences and those of the Grays became one and the same.

At the end of May 1918, the division went to Camp Lee, near Petersburg, Virginia, where its ranks were filled to strength with draftees. On June 22, the First and Second Battalions, 148th Infantry, sailed from Newport News in a convoy of six troopships and four escorts. The First Battalion, now commanded by Captain Conelly, sailed on the transport *Susquehanna*. The ship arrived at Brest, France, thirteen days later.[35]

After spending four days at Brest, the battalion moved on to Blevaincourt, where the men underwent intensive training that consisted of close-order drill, battle formations, and bayonet practice. They also got the opportunity to throw live grenades and practice shooting rifle grenades. Just as important was the soldiers' introduction to French culture. They learned to eat French cheese and drink French *vin rouge* and *vin blanc* (which the men referred to as "vinegar blink"). Here, too, the men had their first dealings with "Madelon," the stereotypical French café girl. Benson Shupe wrote, "I'm glad I studied French at Shaw High School, the French girls are peaches." On the other hand, George Conelly, brother of Ludwig S. Conelly, wrote, "I have heard much of pretty French girls. If there are any they must be hidden. I have seen none."[36]

The novice soldiers were itching to get to the front, and even Captain Conelly wrote home, "I want to get into the thick of this affair, as soon as possible." They soon got their wish, when, at the end of July, the division was ordered to proceed to Baccarat and take over the trenches in that sector. On the morning of July 28 the First Battalion took up positions in the trenches of the western front. The battalion relieved the First Battalion, 305th Infantry, 77th Division. In order to familiarize the "rookie" Ohioans, the 305th remained with them until August 4. The First Battalion remained in the trenches at Baccarat until relieved two weeks later. The now–trench-savvy veterans repaired to the rear for rest and delousing.[37]

There was little time for rest, however, for on September 21 the division was moved up to the Avocourt sector. A week later units of the 37th were going "over the top" in the Meuse-Argonne offensive.[38]

Sheltering himself in a dugout, William Cadwallader described the beginning of the American offensive. "The rats played in the straw in the bunks and ran along the crannies in the walls early that night, but when the barrage began at 11 o'clock they became quiet and disappeared altogether as the guns roared more loudly and the earth shook more violently. No one slept that night. . . . It seemed as if the world was coming to an end."[39]

At 3:30 on the morning of the September 26, the battalion occupied the front-line trenches opposite Montfaucon. Carrying two days' rations, the battalion went into the attack at dawn. No Man's Land was a wilderness of underbrush, rusted wire, crumbling trenches, and shell holes. There was considerable confusion and great difficulty keeping the men in formation, owing to the dense fog and smoke that blanketed the area. Yet except for sporadic machine gun and sniper fire, there was little German resistance. On the second day, however, the Germans began to check the advance with heavy machine gun and artillery fire. Shells were dropping everywhere. Since many were gas shells, orders were given for the men to wear their gas masks at all times.[40]

Acts of personal courage were commonplace, especially when comrades were in trouble. During the Meuse-Argonne offensive, Corporal Sterling B. Ryan of Company B and his squad had been sent to flank a machine gun nest. But after advancing only about two hundred yards, they came under machine gun fire. The corporal and three of his men fell wounded. 2d Lieutenant Albert Baesel, who had joined Conelly's command at Camp Sheridan, asked permission to rescue his wounded comrades. The Company's position was under heavy artillery, machine gun, and rifle fire. To this was added poison gas. Reluctantly, Lieutenant Baesel was given permission to attempt to reach the men. Accompanied by Corporal Walter O'Connell, Lieutenant Baesel worked his way forward to Corporal Ryan. Lieutenant Baesel had just placed the wounded Ryan on his shoulders when they were both killed by enemy fire. Corporal O'Connell also was severely wounded. For his attempt to save the life of Corporal Ryan, Lieutenant Baesel was posthumously awarded the Congressional Medal of Honor.[41]

At dawn on September 29, the already exhausted First Battalion was ordered to attack the town of Cierges with the assistance of fourteen French tanks. The attack came under heavy artillery and machine gun fire. Mustard and phosgene gas rained down on the attacking Americans. In a short time three tanks were destroyed by German shells; the remaining eleven turned around and began moving to the rear.[42]

For five hours the battalion pounded Cierges, which the men had nicknamed "Death Valley." A soldier compared the din of the battle to the "hum of a thousand pneumatic riveters." The battalion suffered 120 casualties at Cierges. Captain Conelly later commented that "Cierges was a death trap." (During the attack Captain Conelly had a close call. A German machine gun began firing at him. One bullet went through his helmet, grazed his cheek next to his right eye and continued on through a sweater he was wearing.) On the afternoon of October 1, the sixth day of the offensive, the First Battalion was relieved by elements of the 32d Division. Throughout the relief maneuver the Germans gassed the American line.[43]

During their six days in the Meuse-Argonne offensive, the First Battalion had 4 officers and 26 men killed, 6 officers and 234 men wounded, and 223 men missing in action. Many of those reported missing had been gassed and returned to their companies after being treated in field hospitals during the next few days. The total number of casualties was 594, or 70 percent.[44]

After only two days' rest the Battalion was ordered to move into the line in the St. Mihiel sector, where they remained until the middle of October. From there the battalion moved on to Belgium by train. Upon arrival in Belgium, the battalion received the good news that Captain Conelly had been promoted to Major. Bad news followed close behind. The battalion had been ordered back to the front. Thus, on the morning of November 1, although harassed by machine gun snipers Major Conelly and his men advanced to the banks of the Escaut River. Shortly after noon the Germans began to shell the American positions.[45]

That night Conelly's men watched the town of Heurne burn. The sky glowed red and orange from the fires started by the German shelling. A soldier counted 240 shells land in and around the town in an hour. The next day the battalion positions were strafed by German aircraft. The German artillery shells that continuously rained down on the battalion's positions were a deadly mixture of high explosive, shrapnel, and poison gas.[46]

The division was preparing to continue its assault beyond the Escaut River when news of the Armistice was received. After the signing of the Armistice, the Battalion moved through Belgium and

France. Each move brought them closer to home. The terror-filled excitement of the trenches was replaced with the irritating tedium of inspections and parades. On November 20, a detachment of the battalion acted as part of the honor guard for King Albert's triumphant return to Brussels. This was followed in January 1919 by a review by General Pershing.[47]

At the beginning of March, after ten months on the western front, Major Conelly's battalion returned to the Port of Brest and, on March 17, boarded the troopship *St. Louis*. As each man walked up the gangplank, Red Cross workers handed him a new pair of socks stuffed with cakes, chocolates, chewing gum, a bun, and a small can of jam. And throughout the voyage home, the YMCA and the Knights of Columbus handed out candy and cigarettes to the men. Twelve days later, the *St. Louis* docked at Hoboken, New Jersey. A delegation from Cleveland, headed by Mayor Harry L. Davis and Captain Henry P. Shupe of the Grays, was waiting in New York to welcome their soldiers home.[48]

The First Battalion was first sent to Camp Mills, New York, and then on home to Ohio. Major Conelly returned to Cleveland on March 28. Officially, on April 21, 1919, after nearly three years of service, the 148th Infantry Regiment was mustered out of federal service. During the First Battalion's service on the western front, 5 of its officers and 66 enlisted men were killed and 11 officers and 279 were wounded in action. Of the 78 Grays of the original Company F who had served on the border and then in Europe, 6 were killed in action and 26 were wounded.[49]

Their service on the western front during World War I marked the last time the Grays would see active service as a unit. Despite the fact that the National Guard Act of 1903 had stripped them of their official military status, the Grays were carried forward into the trenches of France and Belgium by their past service and aggressive leadership.

A meeting was held at the Armory on the evening of May 19, 1919, for the purpose of reorganizing the Grays and making plans for the future. Sixty-five returned members of the Active Company and members of the Veteran's Association discussed the Grays' future and elected Major Ludwig S. Conelly captain.[50]

Epilogue

IMMEDIATELY after their return from France, the Grays began a drive to increase their membership—not only to attract new members but to induce old members into returning—with the recruiting committee adopting the slogan "Once a Gray, Always a Gray!" While some veterans simply no longer wished to be associated with the military, many of the returned soldiers closely identified themselves with their service in the National Guard and with the newly formed American Legion—with those who had shared their experience in France rather than with the Grays who had stayed at home during the World War. Therefore many of the newer members owed their first allegiance to the Guard and not the Grays. In a symbolic gesture, Company B, 145th Infantry, Ohio National Guard was unofficially designated the Cleveland Grays.

Under the leadership of Ludwig S. Conelly, the Grays seemed secure in their role as Cleveland's premier military organization. As before the war, the Grays marched on Washington's birthday and held their annual New Year's Eve Ball. And in June 1919 the Company excitedly announced plans for a European trip.[2]

During the early morning hours of January 26, 1921, fire broke out in the rear of the Armory. The alarm was sounded by National Guardsmen who had stayed late after drill to play cards. By the time the fire department arrived, the wood-framed roof of the stage house and drill hall were engulfed by flames and thick black smoke. The firemen concentrated their efforts on saving the front part of the Armory and keeping the fire from spreading to adjacent buildings.[3]

In the morning, banner headlines cried, "Grays Armory Burned: Plot by Reds is Hinted." Despite this sensational claim, the fire marshal determined that the fire was caused by faulty wiring and not by incendiary armed Bolsheviks.[4]

The front of the building, which housed the meeting or club rooms was spared, but the fire destroyed the stage house and the drill hall. The Grays ultimately decided to rebuild the sections of the Armory destroyed by the fire. However, the need for a large concert hall and stage house was now being questioned. The early 1920s saw the opening of the great theaters at Play House Square and the Masonic Auditorium at East 36th and Euclid. And in 1922 Public Auditorium, which boasted a seating capacity of 11,500, was opened. Even if rebuilt, the Armory could not compete with the size, visual opulence, and seating capacity of these newer facilities. Also, the size of the lot on which the Armory was built restricted expansion. Thus it was decided that the Armory be rebuilt to house units of the National Guard. The Cleveland Chamber of Commerce pledged $135,000 to the project. In return for the money, the National Guard was to have rent-free use of the Armory for fifteen years.[5]

The loss of revenue caused by the fire, the expenses incurred for repairs, and diminished postfire income began slowly to drain the coffers of the Grays' treasury. In October 1923 the Grays borrowed

$75,000 from Society for Savings at 8 percent per annum. To insure the note, the Grays had to give the Armory as collateral. All the organization's energy was now devoted to paying off the debt to Society for Savings.[6]

Despite their seeming absorption into the National Guard, the Grays continued their independent life in spirit and in legal form. Just as in 1837, men continued to find in a military organization a combined outlet for patriotism and sociability. Although a changed military system had removed the opportunity for national service as a group, individual members continued the organization's tradition of service.

During the Second World War, Company B, 145th Infantry, 37th Division served with distinction in the Pacific Theater of Operations, seeing action in New Georgia, New Guinea and the Philippines. In addition to those serving with the 37th Division, other members of the Grays served in each branch of service and in every theater of operation. But not all the Grays served overseas. Many veteran members and "old timers" served on the home front with the Ohio State Guard, or Civil Defense, which had been formed to replace the National Guard units that were fighting overseas. On the afternoon of the catastrophic East Ohio Gas explosion on October 20, 1944, the Grays Company in the State Guard assisted the Cleveland Police Department in cordoning off the area and keeping at bay the curious public.[7]

Service in World War II was followed by individual members serving in Korea, Vietnam, and, more recently, the Persian Gulf War. The Grays have maintained a tradition of representing Cleveland in America's wars.

Local civic service, an important function from the start, has continued as well. The Grays continue to play a colorful role in parades and other public functions and in helping to honor the city's guests. Grays Armory is a center for downtown social life, whose appeal has widened as the Grays opened their ranks to one and all. Members include African Americans, Asians, women, and nonveterans. Even the peace-keeping function has remained relevant, as the law enforcement agencies have practiced on the Grays' pistol range and the Greater Cleveland Peace Officers Memorial Society Pipe Band has rehearsed in the drill hall. Most important of all, the Grays and their Armory have taken on an increasing role in public education in the form of school tours and the establishment of a military museum. Thus, the Grays present to Clevelanders, young and old, a window to the city's rich and diverse history.

Notes

INTRODUCTION

1. Chronicles the apathy in the ordinary militia that resulted in the formation of independent volunteer companies. Marcus Cunliffe, *Soldiers and Civilians: The Martial Spirit in America, 1775–1865*, 177–255, which presents the constitutional organization of the militia and the Militia Act of 1792; Walter Millis, *Arms and Men: A Study in American Military History*, 40–46, which provides general information on the relationship of the army and the militia and their use as police reserves during times of urban violence; and Robert Reinders, "Militia and Public Order in Nineteenth Century America."

Chapter One
"SUCCESS TO THE GRAYS!"

1. James H. Kennedy, *A History of the City of Cleveland*; Julius P. B. McCabe, *Directory For Cleveland and Ohio City 1837–1838*; and W. Scott Robinson, ed., *History of the City of Cleveland*, 35, 39.
2. *Daily Herald and Gazette*, Sept. 22, 1837. On October 24, 1837, the *Daily Herald* reported that nine men had been sentenced to the penitentiary: three for burglary,

three for grand larceny, two for counterfeiting, and one for horse stealing. The City did not begin compiling records of arrests and crimes until 1862.

The original ordinance establishing a City Watch was passed by City Council on December 28, 1836. *Daily Herald,* Jan. 6, 1837. In March 1837 the Mutual Protecting Society, a volunteer organization dedicated to fire fighting, was formed. Ibid., Mar. 10, 1837. The need for a force to bolster the City Watch was made evident during the fall of 1836, when Cleveland and Ohio City fought the so-called "Bridge War." Violence flared over the building of a second bridge across the Cuyahoga River. Built at a crossing further south of the original bridge, it by-passed Ohio City. Residents of Ohio City, resentful of the new bridge, attempted to burn it down but were met by a mob of angry Clevelanders bent on preventing them from doing so. Tempers flared, shots were exchanged, and three men were seriously wounded. Eventually the affair was settled, with the courts deciding that there could be more than one bridge across the Cuyahoga River. See David Van Tassel and John T. Grabowski, eds., *The Encyclopedia of Cleveland History,* 290–91; and William Ganson Rose, *Cleveland: The Making of a City,* 160. Donald Creighton, *A History of Canada: Dominion of the North,* 244–46; Desmond Morton, *A Military History of Canada,* 75

3. Elinor Kyte Senior, *Redcoats and Patriotes: The Rebellions in Lower Canada, 1837–1838,* 7; Morton, *Military Canada,* 75; Creighton, *Canada,* 246.

4. *Daily Herald,* Nov. 8, Aug. 29, 1837.

5. George W. Tibbitts, *A Brief Sketch of the Cleveland Grays,* 7; Gertrude Van Rensselar Wickham, *The Pioneer Families of Cleveland 1796–1840,* 386–87. In 1845 Ingraham returned to New Bedford, where he continued to serve in the independent militia. At the outbreak of the Civil War, he was elected captain of the New Bedford City Guards and commanded them for three months. Eventually, he would rise to the rank of colonel and command the 38th Massachusetts Volunteer Infantry. Ingraham died in 1876. *Daily Herald,* Feb. 16, 1838.

6. *Daily Herald,* Aug. 29, 1937; Wickham, *Pioneer Families,* 342, 560–61; Van Tassel and Grabowski, eds., *Encyclopedia,* 496.

7. *Daily Herald,* Jan. 2, 1838.

8. Cleveland City Guards, By-Laws and Constitution, Article 3 (18 September 1837), Grays Armory Archives, Cleveland, Ohio.

9. Ibid.; Cleveland City Guards, Records (Sept. 18, 1837), 37; McCabe, *City Directory, 1837–1838,* 90; *United States Census,* 1840, Ohio, microfilm, Western Reserve Historical Society, Cleveland.

10. Cleveland City Guards, Resolution, Sept. 6, 1837; *U.S. Census* (1840); McCabe, *City Directory, 1837–1838.*

11. Guards, By-Laws, Article 4.

12. Guards, Records, Oct. 2, 1837; June 7, 1838, 38.

13. Sometimes during Ingraham's illness, another group of citizens interested in

military training decided to form another independent company. This new company named themselves the Cleveland City Guards. Undoubtedly, because of this imitation, it was decided that Ingraham's Company would change its name. Orlando J. Hodge, "Cleveland Military," 518–19; Guards, Records, June 7, 1838, 38.

14. Creighton, *Canada*, 246; Tibbitts, *Grays*, 8; *Daily Herald*, Nov. 29, 1838.

15. Cleveland Grays, Records, Dec. 24, 1838, 42, Grays Armory Archives; Works Progress Administration, *Historic Sites of Cleveland: Hotels and Taverns*, 8–12; Grays, Records, Jan. 23, 1839, 43; Hodge, "Cleveland Military," 521.

16. Tibbitts, *Grays*, 10; Hodge, "Cleveland Military," 521.

17. Hodge, "Cleveland Military," 521.

18. Tibbitts, *Grays*, 12; Hodge, "Cleveland Military," 524.

Chapter Two

AN AMERICAN COMPANY

1. Arthur M. Schlesinger, Jr., ed., *The Almanac of American History*, 277–80; John Hope Franklin, *The Militant South, 1800–1860*, ix; Cunliffe, *Soldiers*, 277–80; Seymour Martin Lipset and Earl Raab, *The Politics of Unreason: Right-Wing Extremism in America, 1790–1977*, 50. This theme reoccurs from time to time in American history.

2. Hodge, "Cleveland Military," 524–26; Cunliffe, *Soldiers*, 224, 227. While reporting no local attacks upon the Irish, the newspapers reported violence between Americans and the Irish in other parts of the country. *Cleveland Leader*, Apr. 12, 1854. On the other hand, the organization of the German Guards was viewed differently: "the military spirit exhibited by our German adopted citizens does them much credit."

3. The Company records for 1854–60 are lost. *The Shako*, Oct. 1910.

4. Paddock, born in Herkimer County, New York, in 1814, arrived in Cleveland in 1834 and worked for Nicholas Dockstader in the manufacture of hats. In 1837, together with Dockstader, he joined the Grays. He was a member of the City Council and the Board of Education and was a Mason. His first wife died, and in 1865 he married Miss J. E. DeWolf of Bath, New York. Paddock fathered seven children. He died in 1892 at the age of seventy-six. *Cleveland Plain Dealer*, Jan. 5, 1891; *Leader*, Aug. 21, 1854.

5. *Leader*, Aug. 21, 1854; *Daily Herald*, May 12, 1855, Apr. 14, 1856, May 10, 1860. Boosters of the Democratic party banded together to form Little Giant Clubs. *Daily Herald*, Nov. 19, 1860.

6. *Daily Herald*, Jan. 24, July 5, 1855; Hodge, "Cleveland Military," 528; *Leader*, Aug. 17, 1855. *The Daughter of the Regiment*, an operetta by Gaetano Donizetti, was first performed in Paris on February 11, 1840. It tells the story of an orphaned girl who is raised by a French regiment and becomes a *vivandiere*, or sutler. Ultimately, despite loves and tribulations, she discovers that she is actually of noble birth. Despite her newfound

station, her first love is the regiment. The well-received operetta was first performed in the United States in 1854 and in Cleveland during the spring of 1855. William Ashbrook, *Donizetti and His Operas*, 147–48; Gaetano Donizetti, *The Daughter of the Regiment*, 2; *Plain Dealer*, Apr. 24, 1855.

7. *Leader*, May 5, 1855; Tibbitts, *Grays*, 16. Tibbitts incorrectly dates the execution of Parks as 1856.

8. *Leader*, Jan. 12, 14, 24, 25, 1856; Tibbitts, *Grays*, 16.

9. *Leader*, Mar. 10, 13, 18 and May 27, 1856.

10. *Leader*, June 30, 1856, June 8, 1860; William Boyd, *Cleveland City Directory*, 295; *Shako*, Oct. 1910, 5; Tibbitts, *Grays*, 16.

11. *Leader*, July 11, Oct. 5, 1860.

12. Ibid., Sept. 11, 1860.

13. Schlesinger, *Almanac*, 277.

14. *Leader*, Feb. 16, 1861.

15. Schlesinger, *Almanac*, 277–78.

Chapter Three

FOR GOD, UNION, & GLORY

1. Cunliffe, *Soldiers*, 15; *Leader*, Apr. 13, 1861.

2. James M. McPherson, *Ordeal By Fire: The Civil War and Reconstruction*, 163; *Plain Dealer*, Apr. 15, 1861.

3. Jabez Fitch, born in Cleveland in 1823, practiced law and sold real estate, though he devoted much of his life to public service. Before the Civil War he served as fire chief and U.S. marshal; during the war, as head of the Cleveland militia district, he commanded Camp Taylor and also served in the 19th ovi. At war's end he was elected president of the Cleveland Society for the Prevention of Cruelty to Animals, and in 1875 he was elected lieutenant governor. Fitch died in 1884. Van Tassel and Grabowski, eds., *Encyclopedia*, 407; *Plain Dealer*, Apr. 16, 1861.

4. *Leader*, Apr. 16, 1861.

5. Ibid., Apr. 17–19, 1861; *Plain Dealer*, Apr. 19, 1861.

6. *Plain Dealer*, Apr. 18, 1861.

7. *Leader*, Apr. 19, 1861. The Ydrad Boat Club presented Homer Baldwin and Frank H. Hineman, two of its members who were also Grays, with pistols. In the minutes of the boat club, Homer Baldwin is listed as "gone to War." Marcus A. Hanna, another Gray, was elected captain of the club in 1862. Ydrad Boat Club Records, 1861–62, Manuscript Collection, Western Reserve Historical Society, Cleveland, Ohio; *Official Roster of the Soldiers and Sailors of the State of Ohio in the War of the Rebellion, 1861–1866* 1:9–11 (hereafter cited as *Official Roster Rebellion*).

8. Boyd, *Directory*, 30–127.

9. *Plain Dealer*, Apr. 19, 1861.

10. Ibid.

11. Ibid. Upon entering the service for the state, independent companies were given numerical designations. The 1st OVI was made up of the following: Company A, Lancaster Guards; Company B, Lafayette Guards of Dayton; Company C, Dayton Light Guards; Company D, Montgomery Guards of Dayton; Company E, Cleveland Grays; Company F, Hibernian Guards of Cleveland; Company G, Portsmouth Guards; Company H, Zanesville Guards. Albert Kern, *History of the First Regiment, Ohio Volunteer Infantry in the Civil War, 1861–1865,* 5.

12. *Leader*, Apr. 22, 1861. Colonel Alexander McCook was born in Columbiana County in 1831. He graduated from West Point in 1852 and was assigned to duty in the West with the 3d Infantry Regiment, where he saw action against the Apaches. Upon completing his assignment in the West, he returned to West Point as an instructor of tactics. In 1861 he was commissioned colonel of the 1st OVI. Mark Boatner, *The Civil War Dictionary,* 526–27.

13. *Plain Dealer*, Apr. 22, 1861.

14. Michael J. McAfee and James L. Kochan, "1st and 2nd Ohio Volunteer Infantry Regiment, 1861," 182–83; James L. Kochan, "Notes on Ohio Uniforms, 1861," 84–85. Before the war, Schenck had served in the state legislature and in Congress and had been the U.S. minister to Brazil under President Millard Fillmore. Boatner, *Dictionary,* 725; Whitlaw Reid, *Ohio in the War* 2:806.

15. *Leader*, July 1, 1861; William C. Davis, *Battle at Bull Run: A History of the First Major Campaign of the Civil War,* 36–40; R. N. Johnston, *Bull Run: Its Strategy and Tactics,* 55–56; *The War of the Rebellion: A Compilation of the Official Records of the Union and Confederate Armies,* vol. 2:124–30 (hereafter cited as *OR*).

16. While Maxcy Gregg was also an officer of volunteers, unlike Schenck he had gained some military experience during the Mexican War. He was a lawyer by profession and a leader among South Carolina secessionists. He was mortally wounded at Fredericksburg in 1862. Boatner, *Dictionary,* 58; *OR*, vol. 2:124–30.

17. *Leader*, July 1, 1861; *Plain Dealer,* July 8, 1861.

18. *Plain Dealer*, July 8, 1861.

19. Ibid., July 29, 1861; *Leader*, July 29, 1861; Davis, *Bull Run*, 163–240; Thomas E. Greiss, ed., *Atlas for the American Civil War,* 3.

20. *Leader*, July 29, 1861.

21. Ibid.; *Official Roster Rebellion* 1:1.

22. Boatner, *Dictionary,* 101; *Official Roster Rebellion* 1:1.

23. *Leader*, July 26, 30, 1861; *Plain Dealer,* July 25, 1861.

24. *Leader*, Aug. 8, 1861.

25. Ibid., Aug. 19, Oct. 18, 1861.

26. Ibid., Aug. 5, 1861; *Official Roster Rebellion* 2:14; William C. Stark, "History of the 103rd Ohio Volunteer Infantry Regiment, 1862–1865," 5–6. The Roll of Honor of the Cuyahoga County Soldiers and Sailors Monument lists residents of the county serving in seventy-one different Ohio infantry regiments. Of this number, the headquarters and staff of eighteen regiments were raised in Cleveland: the 1st, 7th, 23d, 27th, 37th, 41st, 60th, 65th, 67th, 84th, 103d, 107th, 124th, 125th, 128th, 129th, 150th, and 177th. William Gleason, *History of the Cuyahoga County Soldiers and Sailors Monument,* 627–762. The entry on Cuyahoga County regiments omitted the 129th. Van Tassel and Grabowski, eds., *Encyclopedia,* 193; Edward Bowers, "The Cleveland Grays: The First One Hundred Years," 18; Tibbitts, *Grays,* 17–22.

27. Reid, *Ohio* 2:484; Tibbitts, *Grays,* 20; *Official Roster Rebellion* 6:628–29; McPherson, *Ordeal,* 159.

28. *OR,* vol. 12, 3:397. During 1862 the 84th ovi was assigned to the railroad district, Department of the Mountains, which was commanded by former railroad agent Brigadier General Benjamin Franklin Kelley. After this period the regiment was assigned to the Eighth Corps, Middle Division. Boatner, *Dictionary,* 450; Van Tassel and Grabowski, eds., *Encyclopedia,* 368.

29. Reid, *Ohio* 2:484; Henry L. Burnham, a native of Kinsman, in Trumbull County, served as a private in Company D. His diary provides interesting details of clothing issue, a typical day in garrison, and receipt of pay. Henry L. Burnham, Diary, June 5–Sept. 7, 1862, pp. 26, 30, Manuscript Collection, Western Reserve Historical Society. Armies on the move needed large supplies of salt to preserve their foodstuffs, especially meat.

30. Burnham, Diary, 17, 30; Reid, *Ohio* 2:484. Ten soldiers are listed as having died of disease during the regiment's term of service. *Official Roster Rebellion* 6:621. Whitlaw Reid places the number of deaths at fourteen. Reid, *Ohio* 2:484.

31. All white male citizens ages eighteen to forty-five were required by law to enroll in the militia. Ohio, *General Regulations for the Military Forces of Ohio with the Laws Pertinent Thereto,* 163; Van Tassel and Grabowski, eds., *Encyclopedia,* 985.

32. Frank Vandiver, *Jubal's Raid: Early's Famous Attack on Washington in 1864,* 123, 139; Benjamin Franklin Cooling III and Walton H. Own II, *Mr. Lincoln's Forts: A Guide to the Civil War Defenses of Washington,* 7, 14; Benjamin Franklin Cooling III, *Symbol, Sword and Shield: Defending Washington During the Civil War,* 157, 184, 186.

33. *Official Roster Rebellion* 9:139. The 150th ovi was composed of Companies A, B, C, D, E, F, G, and H of the 29th Ohio National Guard (ong); and Company I, 30th ong; and Company K, 37th ong, which was composed mostly of students from Oberlin College. William G. Gleason, "History of the 150th Regiment Ohio Volunteer Infantry," Speech Delivered at the 5th Annual Reunion, Scenic Park, Rocky River, Ohio, July 12, 1899, p. 6, Cleveland Public Library.

34. On April 19, 1861, the 6th Massachusetts was attacked by a pro-secessionist mob as they marched through Baltimore on their way to Washington. Nine civilians and four soldiers were killed in the melee. John S. Bowman, ed., *The Civil War: Day by Day*, 28; Gleason, "150th ovi," 7–8.

35. The regiment was deployed in the following manner: two companies at Fort Lincoln; one at Fort Thayer; one at Fort Saratoga; one and a half at Fort Bunker Hill, the other half at Fort Slocum; and one at Fort Stevens. The regimental headquarters was located at Bunker Hill, with the lieutenant colonel at Fort Lincoln and the major, or third in command, at Fort Slocum. *OR,* ser. 2, vol. 37:461, vol. 47:245. In addition, Gleason paces half a company at Fort Slemmer. Gleason, "150th ovi," 8; James C. Cannon, *Record of Service of Company K, 150th Ohio Volunteer Infantry*, 9, 13.

36. Cannon, *Company K*, 9, 10.

37. Gleason, "150th ovi," 9.

38. McPherson, *Ordeal*, 414–22, 428; Geoffrey C. Ward, *The Civil War: An Illustrated History*, 288–90; Vandiver, *Raid*, 59.

39. Boatner, *Dictionary*, 255–56; McPherson, *Ordeal*, 428; Gleason, "150th ovi," 9; *OR,* ser. 2, vol. 37:245–46; Cannon, *Company K*, 16.

40. *OR,* ser. 2, vol. 37:231–32, 246. So great was the emergency that Quartermaster-General Montgomery C. Meigs reported with 1,500 quartermaster employees, whom he armed and equipped and then positioned in and around Fort Slocum. The positions were further reinforced by 2,800 convalescents and men from the military hospitals around Washington. Cooling, *Symbols*, 194.

41. McPherson, *Ordeal*, 428; Boatner, *Dictionary*, 255–56; *OR,* ser. 2, vol. 37:232.

42. *OR,* ser. 2, vol. 37:237; *Official Roster Rebellion* 9:141–54. Stacking arms involved turning in the weapons issued by the state; when called back to duty, the men were reissued weapons and equipment. Gleason, "150th ovi," 15; *Leader,* Aug. 16, 1864; Reid, *Ohio* 2:681.

43. Gleason, "150th ovi," 19.

44. Ibid.

45. *Leader,* Apr. 29, 1865; McPherson, *Ordeal*, 482–83; Van Tassel and Grabowski, eds., *Encyclopedia*, 5.

46. Ibid.

47. Adjutant General Reports, Ohio National Guard Personnel Records by County, 1863–66, Cuyahoga County, 29th Regiment Ohio Volunteer Militia, State Historical Society Archives, Columbus.

Chapter Four
PROTECTORS & POLICEMEN

1. Barton C. Hacker, "The United States Army as a National Police Force: The Federal Policing of Labor Disputes, 1877–1898,"; State of Ohio, *Annual Report of the Adjutant General for the Year 1868*, 11. The *City Directory* for 1867–68 gives no listings for military organizations; however, there are forty-three listings for fraternal, benevolent, and temperance-oriented organizations. *Cleveland City Directory 1867–1868*, 543–44.

2. Grays, Records, Sept. 22, 1869, Oct. 7, 1869, 81, 84. John Frazee, born in Wyantskill, New York, in 1829, moved to Cleveland in 1850, and sometime after 1854 he joined the Grays. During the Civil War he served in Company E, 1st OVI, in the 84th OVI, and in the 150th OVI. In 1867 he was appointed the first chief of the Cleveland Police Department. He served as president of the Grays from 1870 to 1885. He died in 1917. Van Tassel and Grabowski, eds., *Encyclopedia*, 260, 421; *Shako*, Sept. 1910.

3. Grays, Records, Oct. 1, 14, 1869, 82, 85.

4. The Standing Committee—composed of three appointed members, the commander, and the recording secretary—had "a general supervision of the affairs of the Company." The committee made all contracts on behalf of the Company, was responsible for financial affairs, and received and reported all applications for membership. Grays, Code of Laws, Article 9 (Oct. 1869), 65; Grays, Records, Oct. 1–Dec. 31, 1869, 82–95.

5. The 1869 roster included the following names: Charles Burgess, bookkeeper; Max Gebhardt, salesman; Emery Hessler, botanical druggist; T. Arthur Kelley, engineer; Harvey Laughlin, bookkeeper; John T. McGuinnes, bookkeeper; George McIntosh, clerk; Charles Murfey, bookkeeper; William Murfey, bank clerk; Charles F. Quinlin, clerk; Arthur H. Quinn, partner in A. Quinn and Sons flour millers; and William L. Hasseldt, salesman. Grays, Records, Oct. 1–Dec. 31, 1869; *Cleveland City Directory 1868–1869*, 181–262.

6. Grays, Records, Oct. 21, Nov. 1, 1869, 86, 87.

7. *Leader*, Dec. 29–Dec. 30, 1869.

8. Louis Adamic, *Dynamite: A Story of Class Violence in America*, 3.

9. Reinders, "Militia," 87–88.

10. Adamic, *Dynamite*, 25–28.

11. Ibid., 31.

12. Ibid., 29; Ohio, Adjutant General Reports, Miscellaneous Telegraph Dispatches, Railroad Strike 1877 (July 21, 1877), State Historical Society Archives. The Lake Shore and Michigan Railroad shop men struck for a raise from 19 cents to 21 cents per hour for a ten-hour day. The Union depot freight handlers demanded $1.50 for a ten-hour day and $2.00 for Sundays and also requested overtime and to be paid by the 15th of each month. In addition, the strikers wanted assurances that no one would be fired for participating in the strike. *Leader*, July 24, 1877.

13. Robert V. Bruce, *1877: Year of Violence,* 203–5.

14. Letter to Barnett from Mayor W. G. Rose, Apr. 21, 1877, James Barnett Papers, Western Reserve Historical Society. Barnett joined the Grays in 1837 and two years later became a member of the gun squad. In 1845 he became active in the Cleveland Light Artillery. During the Civil War he commanded the 1st Ohio Light Artillery, serving with distinction at Shiloh and Nashville. He was brevetted to the rank of brigadier general and appointed to the post of chief of artillery on the staff of General Rosecrans. Barnett claimed the distinction of having held the highest rank of any soldier from Cuyahoga County who served in the Civil War. After the war he became president and chairman of the board of the George Worthington Company and later became president and chairman of several other local banks and of the Cleveland Iron Mining Company. Van Tassel and Grabowski, eds., *Encyclopedia,* 77.

15. Mortimer D. Leggett commanded the 78th Ohio ovi and saw action at Fort Donelson, Shiloh, Vicksburg, and Champion Hill and participated in Sherman's March to the Sea. He rose to command the Third Division, Seventeenth Corps, and was appointed major-general in January 1865. After the war he settled in Cleveland and established a practice as a patent attorney. He served on the Board of Education and on the Soldiers and Sailors Monument Commission. Reid, *Ohio* 1:311; *Plain Dealer,* Jan. 7, 1896; *Leader,* Jan. 10, 1896; letter to Barnett from Mortimer D. Leggett, Aug. 1877, Barnett Papers. The First City troop was the forerunner of Troop A, 107th Cavalry Regiment, Ohio Army National Guard. Alfred Mewett, *A Brief History of Troop A,* 7. The unit boasted two Gatling Guns. While alerted on several occasions, they never fired their guns in anger. When the company disbanded in 1905, their property, including the two guns, was turned over to the Grays. Van Tassel and Grabowski, eds., *Encyclopedia,* 235; Grays, Records, Feb. 1–28, 1905. With the exception of a few photographs and miscellaneous documents in the Grays Armory collection, the Gatling Gun Company property, including the two guns, has been lost.

16. *Reports of the Departments of the Government of the City of Cleveland for the Year Ending December 31, 1878,* 45; James W. Whipple, "Cleveland in Conflict: A Study in Urban Adolescence, 1876–1900," 93–94; *Leader,* Oct. 30, 1879; Grays, Records, June 7, 1880, 409.

17. Grays, Records, Sept. 22–Dec. 31, 1869, 83–95, and Jan. 1–Dec. 31, 1876, 274–309; Grays, Miscellaneous Papers and Programs (Minstrel Program, 1886); Ibid. (5 October 1896).

18. Ibid. (5 April 1878)

19. The workers' demands included: management's acceptance of a wage scale set up by the union; a closed shop for skilled workers; consultation with the union before the discharge of a member; and the reinstatement of some recently fired workers. Henry B. Leonard, "Ethnic Cleavage and Industrial Conflict in Late 19th Century America: The Cleveland Rolling Mill Strikes of 1882 and 1885," 528, 531. Mayor Herrick invoked Statute 3096 of the Ohio Revised Statutes, which stated that in time of "tumult, riot or

mob" a mayor may issue a call to the militia in order to prevent crime and the destruction of property and/or to bolster civil authority. *Ohio Statutes* (1880) 1:792. Grays, Records, June 14, 1882.

20. Ibid., June 26, 1882; Leonard, "Strikes," 536; Van Tassel and Grabowski, eds., *Encyclopedia*, 270.

21. Leonard, "Strikes," 528, 536–37; *Leader,* July 7, 1885. Ironically, many of the unskilled Eastern European strikers of 1885 had been scabs in the dispute of 1882.

22. *Leader,* July 8, 1885; Leonard, "Strikes," 547; Van Tassel and Grabowski, eds., *Encyclopedia*, 270.

23. *Leader,* July 8, 1885.

24. Ibid.; Grays, Records, Aug. 6, 1885, 115.

25. Grays, Records, Aug. 6, 1885, 115; Van Tassel and Grabowski, eds., *Encyclopedia*, 271.

26. Rose, *Cleveland,* 572, 597; Grays, Records, July 24, 1899, 67; *Plain Dealer,* July 26, 1899.

Cahpter Five
IT'S FUN TO BE A SOLDIER

1. This was the first public appearance of the Gatling Gun Company. Grays, Records, Sept. 10, 1879, 10.

2. Ibid.

3. Ibid., Aug. 13, 1877, 210; July 15, 1878, 290; July 31, 1879, 338; and July 3, 1882, 98. Grays, Special Order 8 (July 29, 1887) and Special Order 16 (July 14, 1890); *Leader,* July 11, 1885.

4. Grays, General Order 61 (Aug. 1, 1887); Bowers, "Grays," 29.

5. *Leader,* Aug. 11, 1885. Both Marcus Hanna and Myron T. Herrick had been members of the Grays. Hanna served as a lieutenant with the 150th OVI during the Civil War; Herrick joined the Grays in 1878. Grays, Records, Apr. 22, 1878, 260.

6. Grays, General Order 1 (July 24, 1880); *Leader,* July 9, 1879.

7. *Leader,* July 9, 1879.

8. Ibid. The trip to Lakewood at Lake Chatauqua cost the Grays $2,195 in 1887. Each man was assessed $10; three years later the same trip cost $2,800 and each member's assessment was increased to $15. Grays, Records, June 27, 1887, 65; Aug. 2, 1887, 76; June 9, 1890, 277.

9. Ibid., Nov. 8, 1880, 443. Dan Parmellee Eells was a Cleveland banker and financier who held interests in oil refineries, iron and steel companies, cement manufacturers, coke and gas works, and railroads. He was also active in a number of philanthropic causes, including the Cleveland Bible Society, the YMCA, and the Children's Aid Soci-

ety. In 1880 he founded the Bucyrus Steam Shovel and Dredge Company. He died in 1903. Van Tassel and Grabowski, eds., *Encyclopedia*, 367; Grays, Records, Feb. 21, Mar. 7, 1881, 462, 470.

10. *Leader*, Mar. 5, 1881. Cleveland's independent cavalry unit, the First City Troop, also participated in the inauguration. Grays, Records, Mar. 7, 1881, 464; Bowers, "Grays," 25.

11. Peskin, *Garfield*, 596, 607.

12. Ibid., 608–9; Bowers, "Grays," 27; *The Man and the Mausoleum: Dedication of the Garfield Memorial Structure*, 79, 92.

13. Grays, Records, Mar. 11, 1889, 185; *Leader*, Mar. 4, 1889.

14. Bowers, "Grays," 36; *Leader*, Mar. 4, 1889.

15. Grays, Records, Feb. 4, Mar. 11, 1889, 184, 185. The trip cost the Grays $5, 329. More affluent, the Grays treasury paid for most of the expenses; the remainder was donated. Bowers, "Grays," 36.

16. Bowers, "Grays," 39; *Cleveland World*, Oct. 23, 1892. A Chicago reporter complimented the Grays in classic nineteenth-century prose: "These Cleveland Grays are men of worth. They can do a full days march; then they can bivouac and be gay. They can obey the Governor's call and go forth to maintain the peace, or do battle for their state's weal and welfare. They have done it these Cleveland Grays." *Chicago Times*, Oct. 22, 1892.

17. Bowers, "Grays," 49; Grays, Records, July 2, 1883, 178; July 20, 1897, 347.

18. Grays, Records, Mar. 14, 1895, 266–67; Bowers, "Grays," 49. Members traveling to New Orleans were assessed $25 for the cost of the trip. Non-members, or "outsiders," were charged $40. Grays, Records, Jan. 23, 1895, 255; Jan. 14, 1895, 250.

19. Captain Henry P. Shupe expressed these feelings: "While I am in command I want the Grays to break their record for trips. The California journey will do it. This will be the greatest trip the Company can make in this country. If any of my successors in command want to outdo it they will have to take the Company to Europe." *World*, June 11, 1902.

20. Grays, Records, May 6, 27, 1902, 129, 130; Jan. 6, 1903, 143; May 30, 1903, 149; *Plain Dealer*, May 3, 1903; *Leader*, May 6, 1903; Bowers, "Grays," 50; *Leslie's Weekly*, May 28, 1903, 5.

21. Grays, Records (30 May 1903), 149.

22. Ibid., 150; Major General William Rufus Shafter was commander of land operations in Cuba during the Spanish-American War. Maurice Matloff, ed., *American Military History*, 328.

23. Grays, Records, May 30, 1903, 150, 151.

24. Ibid., Nov. 5, 1906), 254; Sept. 14, 1908, 302; Mar. 15, 1908, 291. The train consisted of six Pullman sleepers, two dining cars, one combination baggage and assembly car, a kitchen car, and an equipment car.

25. Grays, Records, Mar. 15, 1908, 291; *Savannah Morning News,* Feb. 25, 26, 1908.

26. *Savannah Morning News,* Feb. 25, 1908; Bowers, "Grays," 51, 52. Bowers is incorrect when he places the Grays' visit to Savannah after their return from Cuba.

27. Harry Gilchrist was elected to the Grays on January 7, 1895. He was commissioned in the medical corps of the regular army in July 1898. Grays, Records, Jan. 7, 1895, 245; Ralph D. Cole and W. C. Howells, *The Thirty-Seventh Division in the World War, 1917–1918* 1:63; Grays, Records, May 30, 1908, 312.

28. Bowers, "Grays," 51; Grays, Scrapbook, *Augusta Chronicle,* Mar. 7, 1908. John D. Rockefeller was an Honorary Member of the Grays. Grays, Records, Nov. 6, 1893, 145.

29. Bowers, "Grays," 52; Grays, Records, May 30, 1908, 303.

30. Thirty Grays and seventy guests traveled to Mexico in 1910; two years later the Grays returned to the Pacific Coast and the Canadian Rockies; in February 1913 the Grays appointed a committee to begin planning a trip to Europe for the summer of 1914. Grays, Records, Apr. 4, 1910, 14; Sept. 9, 1912, 60–63; Feb. 10, 1913, 74.

31. Letter Soliciting Support to Build a Grays Armory, July 1888, Barnett Papers.

32. *Leader,* Dec. 9, 1892; Bowers, "Grays," 37.

33. *Leader,* Dec. 9, 1892; Bowers, "Grays," 37.

34. *Leader,* Dec. 9, 1892. The remnants of the flag taken from the ruins are on display in Grays Armory. Company property destroyed in the fire included: all equipment, uniforms, 140 bearskin shakos, 125 rifles, and the colors. In addition, Companies A, B, and F, 5th Regiment, ONG, and the Cleveland Light Artillery lost all their property.

35. *Leader,* Dec. 9, 12, 1892; Grays, Records, Dec. 8, 1892, 78.

36. Grays, Records, Dec. 16, 27, 1892, 82, 83.

37. Ibid., Jan. 3, 1893, 86; Jan. 30, 1893, 92; Jan. 5, 1893, 112. The shakos cost the Grays $3,702, or $29.66 each. Ibid., July 3, 1893, 114.

38. The vote was 54 ayes and 10 nays. Grays, Records, July 3, 1893; May 1, 1893, 108.

39. Ibid., Apr. 7, 1893, 102; May 1, 1893, 108; Grays, Membership Certificates of Indebtedness (1894), 1–75. Grays Armory Archives, Cleveland, Ohio. In December 1893 the Company borrowed $15,000 from the Citizen's Savings and Loan Association (7 percent interest per annum) for building purposes. Records do not exist for the actual cost of the completed building; however, in 1894 the Armory and its contents were insured for $31,500. Grays, Records, Dec. 4, 1893, 151.

40. Grays, Records, Nov. 6, 1893, 145; Van Tassel and Grabowski, eds., *Encyclopedia,* 1045; *Leader,* Aug. 4, 1909.

41. Grays, Records, Nov. 6, 1893, 145; Van Tassel and Grabowski, eds., *Encyclopedia,* 486, 578–79, 1045–46.

42. *Plain Dealer,* May 31, 1893; Grays, Records, May 1, 1893; *Leader,* May 31, 1893.

43. *Leader,* May 31, 1893; Grays, Records, Dec. 4, 1893, 151.

44. The galleries were filled with hundreds of friends, guests, and family members who had come out to wish the Grays and their new home well. *Leader,* Feb. 13, 23, 1894.

45. Grays, Records, Feb. 5, 1894, 161; Oct. 1, 1894), 219.

46. Ibid., Dec. 7, 1894, 239; *World,* Feb. 2, 1905; *Cleveland Press,* Nov. 1, 1905.

47. Clay Herrick, "Grays Armory Is Built Like a Medieval Fortress," 16–17; *Plain Dealer,* Apr. 6, 1914.

48. Grays, Records, Apr. 2, 1894, 174. In 1892 and 1893 the military company was reorganized. The Active Company consisted of the following officers: one captain, one senior 1st lieutenant, one junior 1st lieutenant, one senior 2d lieutenant, one junior 2d lieutenant. The staff included an adjutant, judge advocate, quartermaster, commissary officer, inspector of the rifle practice, surgeon, and chaplain. Warrants were issued for the following noncommissioned officers: one sergeant-major, one 1st sergeant, eight duty sergeants, two color sergeants, and eight corporals. Grays, Records, Dec. 5, 1892, 76; Jan. 3, 1893, 87; Apr. 2, 1894, 174–76.

The Company posted a list of "Armory Rules of Conduct": (1) The rooms of the Armory shall be open to members only; (2) No one is allowed in the Club Rooms except as an invited guest; (3) No wine, ale, beer, spirituous, or intoxicating liquor of any description shall be allowed in or about the Club Rooms or Armory; (4) No gambling will be allowed; (5) No equipment or property will be removed without written permission of the Quartermaster. Rules 1, 2, and 5 were strictly adhered to; 3 and 4, however, were discreetly ignored. Ibid., 178.

Chapter Six
CRITICS & CUBA

1. Cunliffe, *Soldiers,* 274; Charles A. Peckham, "The Ohio National Guard and Its Police Duties," 56; Adjutant General, State of Ohio, *Annual Report* (1895), 71–74.

2. Peckham, "Police," 56; *Leader,* Oct. 5, 1895.

3. Adjutant General, *Annual Report* (1895), 74.

4. *Leader,* Dec. 10, 1892; Grays, Scrapbook, *Penny Press* Clipping (n.d.).

5. Matloff, *Military History,* 322.

6. Paul Revere, *Boys of '98: A History of the Tenth Regiment Ohio Volunteer Infantry,* 2; Paul Revere, *Cleveland in the War with Spain,* 249; *Plain Dealer,* Mar. 23, 24, 27, Apr. 8, 10, 1898; Grays, Records, Apr. 4, 1898, 42.

7. *Plain Dealer,* Mar. 27, 1898; Revere, *War with Spain,* 166; *Plain Dealer,* Mar. 27, 1898; Grays, Scrapbook, *Penny Press* clipping (n.d.).

8. Grays, Records, Apr. 21, 1898, 44; *Leader,* Apr. 22, 1898.

9. *Leader,* May 26, 1898; Grays, Records, May 30, 1898, 50. The 10th Ohio was a

composite regiment that consisted of three companies of engineers, three batteries of light artillery, four divisions of naval militia, and two unattached companies. Adjutant General, *Report* (1898), 7.

Colonel Kingsley had been a member of the Grays from 1880 to 1889; in June 1898 he was appointed Adjutant General by Governor Bushnell. Revere, *War with Spain*, 16; Grays, Records, June 18, 1898, 50; Revere, *Boys*, 41. Otto Schade replaced Major Arthur B. Foster as battalion commander. A veteran of the Civil War, Foster felt that he had already put himself in harm's way for his country and that as the head of several businesses "his first and important duty is at home." *Plain Dealer*, June 25, 1898; Grays, Records, Apr. 21, 1898, 44.

After the Spanish-American War, James R. McQuigg resigned from the Grays but remained on duty with the Engineers. He commanded the 112th Engineer Battalion, 37th Division, in France during World War I. After the war he became active in the American Legion and in 1925 was elected National Commander. Also active in local politics, he served as mayor of East Cleveland. Van Tassel and Grabowski, eds., *Encyclopedia*, 653; Revere, *War with Spain*, 256, 259, 261; idem, *Boys*, 44–45.

10. Grays, Records, June 18, 1898, 50; *Plain Dealer*, June 26, 1898.

11. Ibid.

12. *Leader*, Aug. 2, 1898. On January 8, 1898, as recognition of service to the city during times of strife and unrest, the City Council passed a resolution to place the janitor at Grays Armory on the city payroll at fifty dollars per month. City of Cleveland, Council Proceedings, Jan. 8, 1894, p. 212, City Hall Archives; *Leader*, Aug. 6, 1898.

13. *Leader*, Aug. 6, 1898. Major Foster was the secretary and general manager of the Cleveland Electrical Manufacturing Company. *Cleveland Directory, 1898*, 350; *Leader*, Apr. 4, 1898.

14. Revere, *Boys*, 10–11; Matloff, *Military History*, 324. The receipt of substandard contract goods was a common and almost expected occurrence. "It is probable that the shoes given to the men will not be given high commendation. Their chief quality has been the remarkable rapidity with which they wore out." *Leader*, July 22, 1898; Revere, *Boys*, 11.

15. Revere, *Boys*, 49, 52, 53; Stephen A. Sted (Stedronsky), interview by author, May 25, 1978, Grays Armory Archives. Stephan A. Sted was the last surviving member of the original Battalion of Engineers. He died at the Brecksville Veterans Hospital on October 23, 1979, at the age of ninety-eight. *Plain Dealer*, Oct. 25, 1979.

16. Revere, *Boys*, 51–56.

17. Ibid., 56–59.

18. 1st Lieutenant Harry W. Morgenthaler was originally assigned to Company A of the Engineer Battalion but was appointed regimental quartermaster on September 28, 1898. After the war, he resigned from the Grays in order to remain with the Engineers. Revere, *War with Spain*, 253; Revere, *Boys*, 58, 59.

19. Sted interview.

20. *Leader,* Apr. 24, May 15, 1899; Grays, Records, May 29, 1899, 61.

21. *Plain Dealer,* July 12, 1899.

22. Grays, Records, Aug. 29, 1899, 97.

23. Grays, Scrapbook, *Penny Press* clipping (n.d.).

Chapter Seven

MEXICO & THE MEUSE-ARGONNE: LAST ACTIONS

1. John Garry Clifford, *The Citizen Soldiers: The Plattsburg Training Camp Movement, 1913–1920,* 5.

2. Charles F. W. Dick served as an officer in the Ohio National Guard during the Spanish-American War. George W. Knepper, *Ohio and Its People,* 331; Clifford, *Citizen Soldiers,* 5, 8, 9; Millis, *Arms,* 161. In 1912 Attorney General George W. Wickersham decided that it was unconstitutional to order the National Guard beyond the borders of the United States. David G. Thompson, "Ohio's Best: The Mobilization of the Fourth Infantry, Ohio National Guard in 1917," 38.

3. Statute 398, *Ohio Statutes* (1904) 97:477.

4. Grays, Records, July 11, 1910, 18; *Shako,* Aug. 1910, 1–7; *Cleveland News,* Apr. 14, 1910.

5. A. J. P. Taylor, ed., *History of World War I,* 21–24.

6. Ibid., 79–81; Clifford, *Citizen Soldiers,* 53.

7. Clifford, *Citizen Soldiers,* 70–71.

8. Grays, Records, Sept. 1, 1903, 158; Oct. 5, 1914, 112; Program, Testimonial Dinner Honoring General Ludwig S. Conelly, sponsored by the Walton Hills Men's Club, Jan. 7, 1963, Conelly Collection, Bedford Historical Society, Bedford, Ohio.

9. Grays, Records, Jan. 4, 1915, 118; Nov. 2, 1914, 114; *Plain Dealer,* July 18, 1915. For the Chagrin Falls camp, see *Plain Dealer* coverage from Aug. 25–Sept. 14, 1915; Clifford, *Citizen Soldiers,* 83–87.

10. Clarence C. Clendenen, *Blood on the Border: The United States Army and the Mexican Irregulars,* 118–22, 202–4; Matloff, *Military History,* 355; R. Ernest Dupuy and William H. Baumer, *The Little Wars of the United States,* 128.

11. Dupuy and Baumer, *Little Wars,* 132, 143; Cole C. Kingseed, "The Test for Readiness: The Ohio National Guard and the Mexican Border Mobilization, 1916–1917," 3. The Punitive Expedition would be the army's last horse-cavalry campaign.

12. Cleveland National Guard Units included the 5th Regiment of twelve infantry companies and a machine gun company; the Battalion of Engineers, Troop A; Cavalry and Battery A, Light Artillery. *Plain Dealer,* May 10, 1916; David A. Niedringhaus, "Dress Rehearsal for World War I: The Ohio National Guard Mobilization of 1916,"

43. President Wilson appointed Newton D. Baker secretary of war in early 1916. Van Tassel and Grabowski, eds., *Encyclopedia,* 67.

13. *Dayton Daily News,* June 19, 1916; *Plain Dealer,* June 21, 1916.

14. *Plain Dealer,* June 21, 1916; Grays, Invoice to Grays for Party Ticket to Dayton for 42 Persons from the Pennsylvania Railroad, June 20, 1916 (July 14, 1916).

15. The route of march was Prospect Avenue to East Ninth Street to Euclid Avenue. *Plain Dealer,* June 21, 1916.

16. Niedringhaus, "Rehearsal," 47; *Plain Dealer,* June 22, 1916.

17. Grays, Letter to L. S. Conelly from Major Daniel C. Stearns, June 24, 1916.

18. *Plain Dealer,* June 22, 1916; *Dayton Daily News,* June 22, July 3, 1916; Grays, Letter to L. S. Conelly from Parker Hiss, Assistant Secretary, Cleveland Chamber of Commerce, June 27, 1916. The people of Middletown and the local Boy Scout troop presented Captain Conelly with $457.22. Grays, Accounting Statement, Jan. 1, 1917.

19. *Dayton Daily News,* July 3, 1916; *Plain Dealer,* July 4, 1916.

20. *Plain Dealer,* July 19, 1916; *Leader,* July 20, 1916.

21. James P. Gates, "Soldiers of the Republic: A History of the Third Ohio National Guard Infantry Regiment 1873–1919," 164.

22. Colonel Hubler, an attorney by profession and a member of the Dayton City Club and the Dayton Golf and Country Club, was in a business and social position to enlist support from corporate leaders on a personal level. Ibid., 164–65.

23. *Plain Dealer,* Sept. 3, 1916; Kingseed, "Readiness," 45. The first unit to leave for the border was the 5th Regiment from Cleveland. The First National Guard unit to reach the border was the 1st Illinois Infantry, which detrained at San Antonio on June 30. By July 4 National Guard units from fourteen states were on the Mexican border. Ibid., 14.

24. Kingseed, "Readiness," 45–46.

25. Gates, "Third Ohio," 166, 169, 170; Kingseed, "Readiness," 49; *Plain Dealer,* Nov. 12, Dec. 23, 1916, and Jan. 2, 30, 1917; Clendenen, *Border,* 296.

26. Grays, Letter to Edward M. Bowers, Secretary Cleveland Grays from L. S. Conelly, Jan. 4, 1917; *Plain Dealer,* Feb. 22, 1917; Grays, Letter from Reverend Hugh Birney, Feb. 23, 1917.

27. Grays, Letter from Birney, Feb. 23, 1917.

28. Matloff, *Military History,* 370.

29. *Plain Dealer,* Apr. 1, 1917.

30. Ibid., Apr. 1, 24, 1917.

31. Gates, "Third Ohio," 187; Kingseed, "Readiness," 68, 90.

32. *Plain Dealer,* Oct. 2, 1917.

33. Cole, *Thirty-Seventh Division* 1:116.

34. Grays, Roster Mexican Border Service, n.d.; *Official Roster of Ohio Soldiers, Sailors and Marines in the World War, 1917–1918,* vols. 1–23 (hereafter cited as *Ohio Soldier Roster*).

35. Cole, *Thirty-Seventh Division* 1:394, 395, 2:21.

36. William Cadwallader, *Major Conelly's Frontline Fighters,* 13; *Plain Dealer,* Aug. 9, 1918. Bensen Shupe, a member of Company F, received on October 31, 1918, a commission as a 2d lieutenant and was assigned to the 66th Infantry Regiment, Fifth Division. *Ohio Soldiers Roster* 16:15, 794. Shaw High School is in East Cleveland, Ohio. George Conelly enlisted in Company F and after service on the border was commissioned a 2d lieutenant and assigned to the 332d Infantry Regiment. Ibid., 4:3210. Cadwallader, *Conelly's Fighters,* 14.

37. *Plain Dealer,* Aug. 9, 1918; Cole, *Thirty-Seventh Division,* 2:74, 76; Cadwallader, *Conelly's Fighters,* 15, 17.

38. Cole, *Thirty-Seventh Division,* 2:197.

39. Cadwallader, *Conelly's Fighters,* 21.

40. Ibid., 20–21, 26–27.

41. Ibid.; Cole, *Thirty-Seventh Division* 2:670. Lieutenant Baesel was hastily buried where he fell. In 1926 a French farmer plowing his field unearthed a skeleton with the Basel's "dog tags." In the spring of 1926 his remains were returned to his home in Berea for burial. The Grays, led by Lieutenant Colonel Conelly, acted as honor escort. See *Cleveland Sun Papers,* May 25, 1898; *Plain Dealer,* Apr. 12, 1926; and other unmarked, undated newspapers in the archives of the Berea Historical Society.

42. Cadwallader, *Conelly's Fighters,* 27, 31.

43. Ibid., 31–32, 34; *Cleveland News,* Mar. 29, Apr. 4, 1919. The "hug-me-tight" sweater that Captain Conelly was wearing was knitted by his daughter Marian. The helmet and sweater are now in the collections of the Bedford Historical Society.

44. Cadwallader, *Conelly's Fighters,* 36.

45. The St. Mihiel Salient had been reduced in mid-September by the first American-planned offensive of the war. Matloff, *Military History,* 396–98; Cadwallader, *Conelly's Fighters,* 19, 39, 50. The *Ohio Soldiers Roster* lists the date of Conelly's majority as November 11, 1918, 4:3210.

46. Cadwallader, *Conelly's Fighters,* 53; *Cleveland News,* Mar. 29, 1919.

47. Cadwallader, *Conelly's Fighters,* 58–59, 63, 68.

48. Ibid., 71–73; *Plain Dealer,* Mar. 20, 1919.

49. Cadwallader, *Conelly's Fighters,* 72, 77–81; *Cleveland News,* Mar. 28, 1919; Gates, "Third Ohio," 159. Among the Grays that were killed in action was Captain Henry Shupe, nephew of Grays former president Henry Shupe. Ironically, Captain Shupe was killed by a German mine near Verdun four days after the signing of the Armistice. Bowers, "Grays," 70. Cadwallader, *Conelly's Fighters,* 69. Ludwig S. Conelly remained in the National Guard after the First World War, and in 1927 he was promoted to brigadier general. During World War II he was appointed deputy commandeer of the 37th Division and served with that unit in the Pacific Theater. In 1944 he was relieved of combat duty because of a heart ailment. He was released from the army at the end of the war with the rank of major-general. Upon returning to civilian life, he continued in

real estate sales and development. He founded and developed the suburb of Walton Hills in Southwestern Cuyahoga County. General Conelly died on October 11, 1963. Program, Conelly Testimonial; *Plain Dealer,* Oct. 12, 1963, and Jan. 15, 1919.

50. *Plain Dealer,* May 20, 1919.

EPILOGUE

1. *Plain Dealer,* Feb. 23, 1920, and Oct. 14, 1922; *Cleveland News,* July 8, 1919.

2. Cleveland Grays, Records, June 6, 1919, 146.

3. *Cleveland News,* Jan. 26, 1921.

4. Ibid., Jan. 26, Feb. 3, 1921.

5. Ibid., Jan. 27, 1921. Grays artifacts, uniforms, photographs, and records were undamaged by the fire. Van Tassel and Grabowski, eds., *Encyclopedia,* 664, 771–72, 803; Grays, Records, Feb. 22, 1922, 215; June 5, 1922, 223. 6. Grays, Records, Oct. 7, 1923, 246–47.

7. Knepper, *Ohio,* 388. Nelson Roby, interview by author, Oct. 16, 1989, Cleveland, Grays Armory Archives. Nelson Roby joined the Grays in 1944 and served in the 5th Infantry Regiment, Ohio State Guard, or, as it was later designated, Ohio Military Reserve. Roby is still active in the Grays. Van Tassel and Grabowski, eds., *Encyclopedia,* 357.

Bibliography

BOOKS, ARTICLES, THESES

Adamic, Louis. *Dynamite: A Story of the Class Violence in America.* New York: Viking, 1934.

Ashbrook, William. *Donizetti and His Operas.* Cambridge, England: Cambridge University Press, 1982.

Boatner, Mark A. *The Civil War Dictionary.* New York: David McKay, 1969.

Bowman, John S., ed. *The Civil War: Day by Day.* Greenwich, Conn.: Dorset, 1989.

Bowers, Edward. "The Cleveland Grays: The First One Hundred Years, 1938." TMs. Grays Armory Archives.

Boyd, William. *Cleveland City Directory.* Cleveland: William Boyd, 1857.

Bruce, Robert. *1877: Year of Violence.* Chicago: Quadrangle Books, 1959.

Cadwallader, William. *Major Conelly's Frontline Fighters.* Cleveland: L. S. Conelly, 1919.

Cannon, James C. *Records of Service of Company K, 150th Ohio Volunteer Infantry.* Cleveland: 150th OVI Association, 1904.

Cleare, Egbert. *City of Cleveland and Cuyahoga County.* Philadelphia: Lippincott, 1875.

Clendenen, Clarence C. *Blood on the Border: The United States Army and the Mexican Irregulars.* Toronto: Macmillan, 1969.

Cleveland City Directory 1867–1868. Cleveland: Leader Company, 1867.

Cleveland City Directory 1896–1896. Cleveland: Leader Company, 1868.

The Cleveland Directory 1898. Cleveland, 1897.

Clifford, John Garry. *The Citizen Soldiers: The Plattsburg Training Camp Movement, 1913–1920.* Lexington: University of Kentucky Press, 1972.

Cole, Ralph D., and W. C. Howells. *The Thirty-Seventh Division in the World War, 1917–1918.* 3 vols. Columbus: F. J. Heer, 1926.

Cooling, Benjamin Franklin III. *Symbol, Sword and Shield: Defending Washington During the Civil War.* Shippensburg, Pa.: White Mane, 1991.

Cooling, Benjamin Franklin III, and Walter H. Own II. *Mr. Lincoln's Forts: A Guide to the Civil War Defences of Washington.* Shippensburg, Pa.: White Mane, 1988.

Cooper, Jerry M. *The Army and Civil Disorder: Federal Military Intervention in Labor Disputes, 1877–1900.* Westport, Conn.: Greenwood, 1980.

———. "The Army as Strikebreaker: The Railroad Strikes of 1877 and 1894." *Labor History* 18 (Spring 1977): 179–96.

Creighton, Donald. *A History of Canada, Dominion of the North.* Boston: Houghton, Mifflin, 1958.

Cunliffe, Marcus. *Soldiers and Civilians: The Martial Spirit in America, 1775–1865.* Boston: Little, Brown, 1968.

Davis, William C. *Battle at Bull Run: A History of the First Major Campaign of the Civil War.* Baton Rouge: Louisiana State University Press, 1977.

Donizetti, Gaetano. *The Daughter of the Regiment.* Boston: Oliver Ditson, 1888.

Dupuy, R. Ernest, and William H. Baumer. *The Little Wars of the United States.* New York: Hawthorne Books, 1968.

Franklin, John Hope. *The Militant South, 1800–1860.* Cambridge: Harvard University Press, 1956.

Gates, James P. "Soldiers of the Republic: A History of the Third Ohio National Guard Infantry Regiment 1873–1919." M.A. thesis. The Ohio State University, 1991.

General Regulations for the Military Forces of Ohio with the Laws Pertinent Thereto. Columbus: Richard Nevins, State Printer, 1859.

Gleason, William. *History of the Cuyahoga County Soldiers and Sailors Monument.* Cleveland, 1894.

Greiss, Thomas E., ed. *Atlas for the American Civil War.* Wayne, N.J.: Avery, 1986.

Hacker, Barton C. "The United States Army as a National Police Force: The Federal Policing of Labor Disputes, 1877–1898." *Military Affairs* 33 (Apr. 1969): 255–64.

Hall, Edward F. "National Service and the American Tradition." *Current History* 56 (Aug. 1968): 72–77, 110.

Herrick, Clay. "Grays Armory Is Built Like a Medieval Fortress." *Properties Magazine,* Mar. 1979, 16–17.

Herring, George C. "James Hay and the Preparedness Controversy, 1915–1916." *Journal of Southern History* 30 (Feb. 1964): 383–404.

Hodge, Orlando J. "Cleveland Military." *Annals*. Vol. 3. Cleveland: Early Settlers Association of Cuyahoga County, 1859.

Johnston, R. N. *Bull Run: Its Strategy and Tactics*. New York: Houghton, Mifflin, 1913.

Kennedy, James H. *A History of the City of Cleveland*. Cleveland: Imperial Press, 1896.

Kern, Albert. *The First Regiment, Ohio Volunteer Infantry, 1861–1865*. Dayton: Privately published, 1918.

Kingseed, Cole C. "Test for Readiness: The Ohio National Guard and the Mexican Border Mobilization, 1916–1917." M.A. thesis. The Ohio State University, 1980.

Knepper, George W. *Ohio and Its People*. Kent, Ohio: Kent State University Press, 1989.

Kochan, James L. "Notes on Ohio Uniforms, 1861." *Military Collector and Historian: The Journal of the Company of Military Historians* 33 (Summer 1981): 84–85.

Leonard, Henry B. "Ethnic Cleavage and Industrial Conflict in Late Nineteenth Century America: The Cleveland Rolling Mill Company Strikes of 1882 and 1885." *Labor History* 20 (Fall 1979): 524–40.

Lipset, Martin Seymour, and Earl Raab. *The Politics of Unreason: Right-Wing Extremism in America, 1790–1922*. Chicago: University of Chicago Press, 1978.

McAffee, Michael J., and James L. Kochan. "1st and 2nd Ohio Volunteer Infantry Regiment, 1861." *Military Collector and Historian: Journal of the Company of Military Historians* 38 (Winter 1986): 182–83.

McCabe, Julius P. B. *Directory for Cleveland and Ohio City, 1837–1838*. Cleveland: Sanford and Lott, 1837.

The Man and the Mausoleum: Dedication of the Garfield Memorial Structure. Cleveland, 1890.

McPherson, James M. *Ordeal by Fire: The Civil War and Reconstruction*. New York: Knopf, 1982.

Matloff, Maurice, ed. *American Military History*. Washington, D.C.: Government Printing Office, 1969.

Mewett, Alfred. *A Brief History of Troop A*. Cleveland: Troop Veterans' Association, 1923.

Millis, Walter. *Arms and Men: A Study in American Military History*. New Brunswick, N.J.: Rutgers University Press, 1956.

Morton, Desmond. *A Military History of Canada*. Edmonton: Hurtig, 1985.

Niedringhaus, David A. "Dress Rehearsal for World War I: The Ohio National Guard Mobilization of 1916." *Ohio History* 100 (Winter/Spring 1991): 35–56.

Official Roster of Ohio Soldiers, Sailors and Marines in the World War, 1917–1918. 28 vols. Columbus: F. J. Heer, 1928.

Official Roster of the Soldiers and Sailors of the State of Ohio in the War of the Rebellion, 1861–1865. 12 vols. Akron: Werner, 1893.

Peckham, Charles A. "The Ohio Guard and Its Police Duties, 1894." *Ohio History* 83 (Winter 1974): 51–66.

Peskin, Allan. *Garfield*. Kent, Ohio: Kent State University Press, 1978.

Revere, Paul. *Boys of '98: A History of the Tenth Regiment, Ohio Volunteer Infantry*. Augusta, Ga.: The Chronicle, 1900.

———. *Cleveland in the War with Spain*. Cleveland: United, 1900.

Robinson, W. Scott, ed. *History of the City of Cleveland*. Cleveland: Robison and Crockett, 1887.

Rose, William Ganson. *Cleveland: The Making of a City*. Cleveland: World, 1950.

Reid, Whitlaw. *Ohio in the War*. 2 vols. Columbus: Eclectic, 1893.

Reinders, Robert. "Militia and Public Order in Nineteenth Century America." *Journal of American Studies* 2 (Apr. 1977): 81–101.

Senior, Elinor Kyte. *Redcoats and Patriotes: The Rebellions in Lower Canada, 1837-1838*. Toronto: Canada's Wings, 1985.

Schaefer, James J. "Governor Willian Dennison and Military Preparations in Ohio, 1861." *The Lincoln Herald* 78 (Summer 1976): 52–61.

Schlesinger, Arthur M., Jr., ed. *The Almanac of American History*. New York: Putnam's, 1983.

Stark, William C. "History of the 103rd Ohio Volunteer Infantry Regiment, 1862–1865." M.A. thesis. Cleveland State University, 1986.

Taylor, A. J. P., ed. *History of World War I*. London: Octopus Books, 1973.

Thompson, David G. "Ohio's Best: The Mobilization of the Fourth Infantry, Ohio National Guard, in 1917." *Ohio History* 101 (Winter/Spring 1992): 37–53.

Tibbetts, George W. *A Brief Sketch of the Cleveland Grays*. Cleveland: The Cleveland Grays, 1903.

Todd, Frederick P. "Our National Guard: An Introduction to its History." *Military Affairs* 5 (Summer 1941): 73–86.

Turnbaugh, Roy. "Ethnicity, Civil Pride and Commitment: The Evolution of the Chicago Militia." *Illinois State Historical Society Journal* 72 (May 1979): 111–22.

Vandiver, Frank. *Jubal's Raid: Early's Famous Attack on Washington in 1864*. New York: McGraw Hill, 1960.

Van Tassel, David, and John T. Grabowski, eds. *The Encyclopedia of Cleveland History*. Bloomington: Indiana University Press, 1987.

The War of the Rebellion: A Compilation of the Official Records of the Union and Confederate Armies. 128 vols. Washington, D.C.: Government Printing Office, 1880–1901.

Ward, Geoffrey C. *The Civil War: An Illustrated History*. New York: Knopf, 1990.

Watson, Richard L., Jr. "Congressional Attitudes Toward Military Preparedness, 1829–1835." *Mississippi Valley Historical Review* 34 (Mar. 1948): 611–36.

Whipple, James W. "Cleveland in Conflict: A Study in Urban Adolescence, 1876–1900: Ph.D. diss. Western Reserve University, 1951.

Wickham, Gertrude Van Rensselar. *The Pioneer Families of Cleveland 1796–1840*. Vol. 2. Cleveland: Evangelical, 1914.

Works Progress Administration. *Historic Sites of Cleveland: Hotels and Taverns*. Columbus: The Ohio Historical Records Survey Project, 1942.

MANUSCRIPT COLLECTIONS

Barnett, General James. Papers. 1845–1906. Manuscript Collection. Western Reserve Historical Society, Cleveland, Ohio.

Burnham, Henry L. Diary. 5 June–Sept. 7, 1862. Manuscript Collection. Western Reserve Historical Society, Cleveland.

Cleveland City Guards. Grays Armory Archives. Grays Armory, Cleveland, Ohio.

Cleveland Grays. Grays Armory Archives. Grays Armory, Cleveland, Ohio.

Conelly, Ludwig S. Collection. Bedford Historical Society, Bedford, Ohio.

Herrick, Myron T. Papers, 1880–1935.

Ydrad Boat Club Records, 1861–62.

The Shako. May 1910–Apr. 1911. Grays Armory Archives. Grays Armory, Cleveland, Ohio.

NEWSPAPERS AND MAGAZINES

Cleveland Herald and Gazette

Cleveland Leader

Cleveland Plain Dealer

Cleveland News

Cleveland Press

Cleveland Sun Papers

Cleveland World

Chicago Times

Dayton Daily News

Leslie's Weekly

Savannah (Georgia) Morning News

Index